STUDIES IN HISTORY
ECONOMICS AND
PUBLIC LAW

**EDITED BY
THE FACULTY OF POLITICAL SCIENCE
OF COLUMBIA UNIVERSITY**

VOLUME THIRTY-EIGHT

CONTENTS

2
ORGANISMIC THEORIES OF THE STATE

ORGANIC THEORIES OF THE STATE

STUDIES IN HISTORY, ECONOMICS AND PUBLIC LAW

EDITED BY THE FACULTY OF POLITICAL SCIENCE OF
COLUMBIA UNIVERSITY

Volume XXXVIII]   [Number 2

Whole Number 101

ORGANISMIC THEORIES OF THE STATE

Nineteenth Century Interpretations of the
State as Organism or as Person

BY

F. W. COKER

AMS Press, Inc.

New York

1967

COLUMBIA UNIVERSITY
STUDIES IN THE
SOCIAL SCIENCES

101

The series was formerly known as
Studies in History, Economics and Public Law.

Reprinted with the permission of Columbia University Press
From the edition of 1910, New York
First AMS EDITION published 1967
Manufactured in the United States of America

Library of Congress Catalog Card Number: 74-120061
International Standard Book Number:
    Complete Set: 0-404-51000-0
    Number 101: 0-404-51101-5

AMS PRESS, INC.
New York, N.Y. 10003

PREFACE

Since the decline of eighteenth-century rationalism in politics many European writers in the fields of political philosophy and public law have interpreted the State as a living entity—as an organism or person. Many recent sociologists, likewise, conceiving society as a living organism, have interpreted the State as a functional system within the social organism. The design of this monograph is to present in general outline the content and setting of these interpretations. The attempt is made to account for the rise and prevalence of such doctrine, to trace its several lines of development, and to suggest certain conclusions as to the validity or consequence of the leading ideas. Though we distinguish two principal tendencies, which we designate as the biological and the psychic, respectively, we use the term organismic to include both tendencies. For, in the first place, the idea of psychic personality is usually in some way associated by its exponents with the idea of organic life; and, in the second place, certain relations of these ideas to a more general conception of organism will be suggested.

An exhaustive canvass of these theories is not attempted. At the same time, the survey is meant to cover the more important nineteenth-century authors in whose theories the organismic conception played a substantial part, and whose interpretations reveal to any significant extent the nature and tendencies of the conception. Some of the less distinctive of these authors are noticed only in foot-note citations.

Reviews of theories which employ the organismic conception in political or sociological interpretation have been made by two earlier monographs. These are Albert Th. van Krieken's *Ueber die sogenannte organische Staatstheorie* (Leipzig, 1873), and Ezra Thayer Towne's *Die Auffassung der Gesellschaft als Organismus, ihre Entwickelung und ihre Modifikationen* (Halle, 1903—a doctoral dissertation by an American student). The latter work considers sociological theories exclusively, and attempts little more than to give successive summary condensations of these. The former was written at too early a date to include the sociologists. It presents a detailed survey of the political writers, and, though giving only a few lines of exposition to each author, it is of great value in the way of bibliographical reference and suggestive classification. At various points guidance has been obtained from these and other monographs, which are duly cited in the foot-notes.

Grateful acknowledgment is also here expressed for the personal aid that has been received in the preparation of this monograph. Professors Charles A. Ellwood and A. O. Lovejoy, of the University of Missouri, contributed useful suggestions as to authors; Professor Henry Jones Ford, of Princeton University, read the greater part of the manuscript and supplied valuable criticism. Finally, the writer is peculiarly indebted to Professor William A. Dunning, of Columbia University, whose supervision and sympathetic counsel in all phases of the work have been indispensable.

F. W. COKER.

PRINCETON, *April, 1910.*

CONTENTS

CHAPTER IV

THE STATE AND THE SOCIAL ORGANISM

CHAPTER V

CHAPTER I

Introduction, Philosophical Basis and Transition

I. INTRODUCTION

In the development of political speculation since the era of the French Revolution there may be differentiated a group of theories which undertake to comprehend the State under the general conceptions of organic life. Though these theories differ from one another in their more practical conclusions and in many aspects of their methods, their common object is to show that the juristic and political character of the State can be truly interpreted only by logically associating it with the ideas of animate nature. Their thesis is that the State is essentially like a natural organism in structure and members, in origin and development; or that it is a higher type of the general class of organic existences within which the animal and vegetable kingdoms form lower types; or that its genesis, nature, and evolution are determined by the laws of the psychic phase, in particular, of the highest type of animal organisms.

At the beginning of this period the prevailing political doctrines were those which were involved in conceptions of a " social contract " and of " natural rights ;" conceptions which had in the two preceding centuries obtained their clearest expression in philosophical treatises, public declarations, and the revolutionary movements. These social-contract theories, while varying much in details, all embodied certain doctrines concerning, on the one hand, man's natural status—from a social and political point of view, and, on the other hand, the status of the State—its origin, its nature and ends, the conditions of its change and betterment, and its relation, as well as that of man, to history. Man's natural position, it was maintained, is that of independence of society and the State. The individual is complete in himself, independent of association with his fellow-men, independent of any necessary relations to a higher unity, independent of the past. He has "natural rights" which are not derived from associate life but may be traced back to the "state of nature" existing prior to the appearance of social or political organization. The State is an institution consciously and voluntarily introduced into the world by man, artificial in its origin, mechanical in its nature and operation. The establishing of a State is a work of pure option, or of mere convenience or prudence. It is a human expedient to avoid various inconveniences, an institution of security. When this State device ceases to fulfill the purposes for which it was instituted it can be artificially reformed from without. What the hands of man have arbitrarily made, can the hands of man arbitrarily demolish and remake. Man can take a position outside of the State, remodel it, discard such parts as do not please him, and evolve a new and untried constitution as a substitute for the old. Men at any period may regard themselves as at the beginning and end of time; may thus, in their theorizing and statesmanship, disregard, on the one hand, the political experience of their fathers, and, on the other hand, take upon themselves to devise a State-structure that will prove acceptable and adequate for those who come after them.

The several lines of theoretical reaction against such
doctrine have been frequently indicated.[1] Their common aim is to displace the individual from his position
of ultimate superiority to the State, as implied in the contract theories, and to ascribe to the State a status of
equal or higher dignity and authority, and of independence of the will or caprice of the individual. The ground
of the existence of the State and the principles of its
change are by them found in some cause superior to, or
at least apart from, human will or desire. By some—
notably De Maistre, De Bonald, and others of the theocratic group of royalist reactionaries in France—the State
is explained as the work of God. The will of God is
the basis and justification of its existence; those institutions which bear the stamp of divine appointment are to
be regarded as sacred and unassailable by man. With
others—the historical school as represented by Burke,
Savigny and others—the explanation of the origin and
nature of the State is found in history. The State is the
slowly evolved product of the work of successive generations of men, the result of the cumulative wisdom of
centuries. Any attempted amendment of the existing
constitution of the State must be correlated with that
past as incorporated in the fundamental laws and customs
of the country; and the renovation must affect "the
peccant part only . . . the part which produced the . . .
deviation"[2] from the dominant course of development.
    But the most direct opposition to the contract dogmas

---

[1] *Cf.* Gumplowicz, *Geschichte der Staatstheorien*, pp. 334 *et seq.;*
Janet, *Histoire de la science politique*, vol. ii, pp. 727–739; Michel,
L'Idée de l'État, pp. 108–168; Merriam, *Theory of Sovereignty since
Rousseau*, pp. 39–43.

[2] Burke, *Reflections on the Revolution in France*, in *Works* (Bohn's
edition), vol. ii, p. 295.

came from those who rejected all assumptions that the State can be determined, in origin and development, by *anything* apart from itself, and maintained that it resists external agencies by a structure and by processes of its own. These theorists held not only that the appearance of the State is independent of human will and invention, but also that the State is a thing of nature, with life, movement, and growth. Its life and growth are peculiar and essential to itself; change or development cannot be imposed upon it from without, but must follow the laws of its own life and evolution.

Notions of a resemblance between the State and living things long antedated the writers of this school; such notions had frequently appeared as incidental suggestions in interpretations which in principle were independent of such comparisons. To indicate particular points of analogy between the State and animals—human beings, in particular—had been a familiar device of illustrative exposition from the earliest times of political philosophy. In the often cited example in the *Republic* of Plato, the reverse process of illustration is followed. Plato sought to attain his explanation of justice as an individual virtue through a definition of public justice. He thus compared the faculties of reason, courage, and sensual desire in man to the ruling-intellectual, warrior, and industrial classes, respectively, within the State. As justice in the State is realized to the extent that each of these classes fulfils its appropriate function—and that function alone— so justice in man is the virtue which maintains order and harmony among the three fundamental human faculties, rendering to each its due, and keeping each within its proper sphere.[1] Similar types of naturalistic compar-

---

[1] This analysis is found in bk. iv of the *Republic*.

ison (the deductions being usually from organic nature
to the State) are common in the writings of the later
classical and early medieval periods.[1]

Otto Gierke, in his *Political Theories of The Middle
Age*, traces, with numerous citations, the prevalence of
this method in later medieval thought, where its applications became more systematic and, in some instances,
more subtle.[2] "Under the influence of biblical allego-
ries," Gierke says, "and the modes set by Greek and
Roman writers the comparison of mankind at large and
every smaller group to an animate body was universally
adopted and pressed."[3] He indicates the employment
of the comparison in the controversies over the relations
between ecclesiastical and temporal authority; each side
displayed some skill in using for its particular purposes
the idea of the necessity of a single head, or of the cor-
respondence of the priesthood to the soul and the
secular realm to the body. With less immediately
polemic object superficial anthropomorphic analogies
were sketched in great detail by John of Salisbury,
Nicholas of Cues, and others.[4] At the same time certain political conclusions of a more general and essential
character were derived by these writers from ideas of a

---

[1] For citations from Aristotle, Cicero, Livy, Seneca, and St. Paul, *cf.*
Krieken, *Die sogenannte organische Staatstheorie*, pp. 19–26; Towne,
Die Auffassung der Gesellschaft als Organismus, pp. 15–24. For dis-
cussion of a more philosophical Greek conception of the organic char-
acter of the State, *cf.* E. Barker, *The Political Thought of Plato and
Aristotle*, pp. 127, 138–9, 276–281, *etc.* For references to examples of
early medieval comparisons, *cf.* Gierke, *Political Theories of the Middle
Age*, notes, pp. 103–4, 112, 122–3, 130 *et seq.*

[2] *Ibid.*, pp. 22–30; notes, pp. 129–137.   [3] *Ibid.*, p. 22.

[4] "John of Salisbury made the first attempt to find some member of
the natural body which would correspond to each portion of the State."
Ibid., p. 24.

fundamental likeness between the State and the "animated body."[1]   Thus such notions as that of the proper apportionment of functions to parts, of the necessary supplementation and intercommunication among these parts, and of the co-ordination of their several operations to a common end, were applied to the State, and attributed to its organic nature.

Later, Hobbes and Rousseau saw analogies to the living organism even in their men-made, contractually established, State.   Hobbes avowedly used the comparison in a somewhat figurative way.   Because human art imitates nature, the State appears to him as an "artificial animal" possessing "artificial life."   The opening paragraph of the Introduction to the *Leviathan* discloses the sense in which Hobbes would combine these seemingly incompatible concepts.

Nature, the art whereby God hath made and governs the world, is by the *art* of man, as in many other things, so in this also imitated, that it can make an artificial animal.   For seeing life is but a motion of the limbs, the beginning whereof is in some principal part within; why may we not say, that all *automata* (engines that move themselves by springs and wheels as doth a watch) have an artificial life?   For what is the *heart*, but a *spring;* and the *nerves*, but so many *strings;* and the *joints*, but so many *wheels*, giving motion to the whole body, such as was intended by the artificer?   *Art* goes yet further, imitating that rational and most excellent work of nature, *man*.   For by art is created that great Leviathan called Commonwealth, or State, in Latin Civitas, which is but an artificial man ; though of greater stature and strength than the natural, for whose protection and defence it was intended ; and in which *sovereignty* is an artificial *soul*, as giving

[1] These ideas appear in the writings of John of Salisbury, Thomas Aquinas, Marsilius of Padua, and other less well known scholastics.

life and motion to the whole body; the *magistrates*, and other *officers* of judicature and execution, artificial *joints; reward* and *punishment*, by which fastened to the seat of the sovereignty every joint and member is moved to perform his duty, are the *nerves*, that do the same in the body natural; the *wealth* and *riches* of all the particular members, are the *strength; salus populi*, the *people's safety*, its *businesss; counsellors*, by whom all things needful for it to know are suggested unto it, are the *memory; equity*, and *laws*, an artificial *reason* and *will; concord, health; sedition, sickness;* and *civil war death*. Lastly, the *pacts* and *covenants*, by which the parts of this body politic were at first made, set together, and united, resemble that *fiat*, or the *let us make man*, pronounced by God in the Creation.[1]

Here and there in the second part—"Of Commonwealth"—animal homologues of organs and parts of the State are briefly instanced.[2]

Not even Rousseau, finally, neglected the resource of naturalistic illustration as a means of enforcing the deductions from his artificial interpretation of State-origin, as set forth in *The Social Contract*. In the chapter on

---

[1] *English Works* (Molesworth edition), vol. iii, pp. ix–x. The italics and capitals are Hobbes's.

[2] For example, the public ministers for general administration resemble "the nerves, and tendons that move the several limbs of a body natural" (p. 227); the ministers for judicature "may fitly be compared to the organs of will in a body natural" (p. 230). Money is the blood of the commonwealth, "the conduits . . . by which it is conveyed to the public use" through the offices of collection and expenditure, being analogous, respectively, to the nerves and arteries of the natural man (pp. 238–9). Colonies are the children of the commonwealth (pp. 239–240). Among the diseases which affect the commonwealth, the infection of democratic teaching produces a disease analogous to hydrophobia (pp. 315–316); the intrusion of the spiritual authority into the affairs of sovereignty, epilepsy (pp. 317–8); a deficiency in public revenues, ague (pp. 319–320). For citations of further examples, cf. Towne, *op. cit.*, pp. 25–7.

"Government," [1] he declares that the "body politic," like the human body, has the two essential "motive powers" (*mobiles*) of "force" and "will," "the latter under the name of *legislative power*, the former under the name of *executive power*." As in man, so in the State, the concurrence of these two powers is a precondition of every voluntary action. Where either endeavors to usurp the sphere of the other, the State falls into dissolution or anarchy. Nevertheless, to the legislative power, as the closer representative of the sovereign people, Rousseau assigns a superior position in the State. To enforce this idea the analogy is somewhat changed: "The legislative power is the heart of the State, the executive power is its brain, which gives movement to all its parts. The brain may become paralyzed and the individual still live. A man remains an imbecile and lives; but as soon as the heart has ceased its functions the animal dies." [2] It is entirely evident, however, that Rousseau was never led by these comparisons far astray from his idea of the fundamental distinction between the State and man. The dominant idea of the *Social Contract*, as of the *Leviathan*, is: "the constitution of man is the work of nature; that of the State is the work of art." [3]

2. CONCEPTIONS PARTIALLY ORGANISMIC

At the time when the results of the frequent overthrowings and reconstructions and arbitrary combinations of States were more directly experienced, the

---

[1] *Du contrat social*, bk. iii, ch. i.

[2] *Ibid.*, ch. xi: "De la mort du corps politique."

[3] *Ibid.* For references to analogies instanced by Fortescue, Bodin, James I, Althusius, Grotius, Pufendorf, and Frederick the Great, *cf.* Dunning, *Political Theories from Luther to Montesquieu;* Merriam, *op. cit.*, and Towne, *op. cit.*

reasoning in reaction from the artificial theories took the form of demonstrating that State-life is real and that the integrity and coherence of the State is a fact.   In other words, to political mechanism was opposed the idea of the essential animateness of the State with its structure of naturally interdependent parts; yet the characteristics of this vitality were not brought into close relation to the forms and conditions of the life of physical organisms.

The argumentation of Adam Müller's *Elements of Politics*,[1] appearing in 1809, is of this type.   This work is devoted largely to a criticism of the contract theories of the eighteenth century.   In its more positive support of an "animate" theory of the State it has to do chiefly with a particular phase of life, namely, that which is manifested in strife and rivalry.   In the State life this is considered to appear most characteristically in war, but to be indicated also in the more peaceful forms of inter-state commercial and cultural contest, as well as in internal competition and other interaction among the members of the State.

The author's constantly recurring idea is that the State is essentially a thing of life and movement, and that only regarded as such can its true nature be apprehended.   This *lebendige Bewegung* is most completely manifested in war.   For here stand out clearly the attributes of life: power and motion; the necessity of organization and inter-connection of parts, of centralization of direction and unity of action, of co-operation of mind, heart, and body; and, finally, contact with other, but similar, living objects.   Müller considers it a striking defect of the current theories of the State that they have in view only the condition of peace and quiet.   "The

---

[1] *Die Elemente der Staatskunst.*

condition of war is as natural as the condition of peace; the State is a militant as well as a peaceful being."[1]

Contact with other States is, however, friendly as well as hostile, and co-operative as well as competitive. A State can no more subsist and develop in isolation from other States than can an individual man fulfil his destiny without knowledge of, or intercourse with, other men. Thus the idea of a universal monarchy is a chimera.

Every State, in order to feel, know, and value itself, needs constantly its like. . . . How might all the innumerable individuals out of which . . . the State arises come to the knowledge that they constitute a whole, if other political groups did not put them in mind of their association and thus impel them to the community which they constitute ? If there is to be one State at all there must be several States and a never-ceasing living intercourse between these States.[2]

But it is not only by intercommunication, rivalry, or conflict with other States that the life of the State is revealed and conditioned. Internal movement and interaction, a harmonizing of diverse aims and interests, are also essential. There must be internal variety. The natural circumstances of a State must be such as to make possible an all-sided development. There must be diversity in climate, topography, and resources, with the consequent diversity in economic and intellectual life.[3] This completeness and multifariousness of physical and cultural elements the author considers to be the chief cause of the greatness of Greece in ancient times and of pre-eminence, among modern States, of France, England, Italy, Spain and Germany.

[1] *Die Elemente der Staatskunst*, p. 13.   [2] *Ibid.*, p. 285.
[3] *Ibid.*, pp. 273-282.

Though Müller combines with his idea of the externally active character of the State a general belief in its
inner vital complexity and integrity, yet the latter notion
is rather subordinate and contributory to the former.
With later writers more emphasis is laid upon the interrelation of the parts of the State and of the dependence
of the parts—the individuals and the minor associations
of individuals—upon the State-whole. The independent
unity and animateness of the State is held to be directly
manifested in its inner structure as well as in its movement. This theory—as applied to society or humanity,
and to man in his relation to society and history, rather
than to the State—received clear formulation at the time
when the eighteenth-century individualistic theories were
in full swing. Herder, Lessing and others set forth the
dependence of the individual upon history and society,
and maintained that the individual is completely himself
only in so far as he fulfils his part in the whole of which
he is an organic element.

Particularly in Herder's philosophy of history[1] is involved the idea that the natural character of man is precisely his quality of being a part of an organically articulated and developing unity. Herder defined *Menschheit*
as a *Zusammenwirkung der Individuen . . . die uns
allein zu Menschen machte.*[2] The history of mankind
has been determined not solely by *Tradition*, but also
through the indispensable *organische Kräfte* of each
generation.[3] The whole cultural development of the
human race has been through the genetic and organic

---

[1] In his *Ideen zur Geschichte der Menschheit*, 1784, *cf.* especially bk. v,
chs. iii–iv and bk. ix, ch. i.   References here are to the Leipsic edition
of 1869, 3 vols.

[2] *Ibid.*, vol. ii, pp. 101 *et seq.*   [3] *Ibid.*, pp. 102–03.

appropriation and conversion by one age of the elements of culture transmitted to it by the preceding ages. The *Ueberlieferung* alone is not sufficient. The generation receiving this *Ueberlieferte* must have the forces and faculties to possess itself of this endowment by assimilating it into its nature. The character of the transformation throughout any period is determined by the peculiar nature of the resolving and assimilating forces of the corresponding generation—by what is taken and the manner in which it is applied and developed. And through all the appearing and disappearing *Menschengestalten* lives continuously the "spirit of mankind" (*Menschengeist*). Only through the view which apprehends this immortal spirit of mankind can the unity and continuity of history be traced through the fragmentary "beginnings without endings" of the successive ages.[1]

3. THE COMBINATION OF CONTRACTUAL AND ORGANISMIC IDEAS

But the transition from the contract to the organismic idea of the State appears perhaps most strikingly in Fichte's *Principles of Natural Right* (1796–97).[2] For though his political philosophy as there set forth is derived from a complex and highly abstract form of the social-contract theory, the essential interdependence of men, as the natural basis of the State, is depicted in

[1] "Die Kette der Bildung allein macht aus diesen Trümmern ein Ganzes, in welchem zwar Menschengestalten verschwinden, aber der Menschengeist unsterblich und fortwirkend lebt." *Ibid.*, p. 106.

"Immer verjüngt in seinen Gestalten, blüht der Genius der Humanität auf und zieht palingenetisch in Völkern, Generationen und Geschlechtern weiter." P. 107.

[2] *Grundlage des Naturrechts.* References here are to vol. iii of *Sämmtliche Werke*, 1845.

terms of organic nature. Schelling said that "the first attempt to construe the State as real organism (*Organization*) was Fichte's *Naturrecht*."[1]

According to Fichte in this work, the State is founded upon a contract—the *Staatsbürgervertrag*—the object of which is the security of all of the members of the State. This agreement is itself made up of three contributory contracts: (1) the negative—"property"—contract by which each pledges his entire assets as a guarantee that he will not injure the property of any of the others;[2] (2) the positive—"protection"—contract by which each obligates himself to assist in the protection of the property of any of the others;[3] and (3) the "union contract" which secures and guarantees the two former contracts and through which is formed the whole (*Ganze*) that is to be protected by the two former contracts.[4] It is just here, in the discussion of the nature of this "whole"— which is the State—that Fichte approaches most nearly the later idea of the State as organic. For, he says, the conception is "not of a mere imagined (*eingebildeten*) whole, which is simply created by our thought, . . . but of a real whole—which is an *Allheit*, not an *Alle*."[5] The uniting fact is the liableness of each to attack; no one knows who may be next threatened; therefore, each makes his contribution to the protecting power, because of the possibility that he himself may become the beneficiary of that protection. The bond of union is thus the uncertainty as to "what individual will need the actual (*sichtbares*) protection and as to whom this protection

---

[1] Schelling, *Vorlesungen über die Methode des Akademischen Studiums*, p. 232.

[2] *Grundlage*, pp. 195-96.   [3] *Ibid.*, pp. 197-98.

[4] *Ibid.*, pp. 198 *et seq.*   [5] *Ibid.*, p. 202.

will potentially (*unsichtbares*) benefit through restraint of the evil will before its outbreak." [1]

Fichte considers that the most fitting figure for making clear the conception of the *totum* thus created and held together is that of the *Naturproduct*—by which he means an object of organic nature.

In the *Naturproduct* each part can be what it is only in its union with the other parts, and out of that union would not be that at all; indeed, out of all organic union it would be nothing, since without the reciprocal action of forces holding each other in equilibrium there would be no enduring form (*Gestalt*) . . . In the same way it is only in the State-union that man maintains a definite position in the series of things, a resting place in nature; and each maintains this definite position against others and against nature only through being in this definite union. [2]

The essential distinction between the citizen and the isolated man is similar to that between the parts of an organic body and the parts of an inorganic body. Every part of the latter has "the ground of its destiny" in itself; its motive (*Trieb*) is completely explained through its existence (*Sein*), and its existence through its motive.[3] Every part of a body of the organic world, on the other hand, has the basis of its destiny outside of itself; its motive presupposes an existence, its existence, a motive, outside of itself. Similarly, the isolated man

acts simply in order to satisfy his own needs, and these are satisfied only through his own actions; what he is externally he is only through himself. The citizen, on the other hand, has to do and to refrain from doing not merely on his own account, but for the sake of others as well; his highest needs

[1] *Grundlage*, p. 208.   [2] *Ibid.*, p. 208.   [3] *Ibid.*, p. 209.

are satisfied through the action of others, without his co-operation (*Zuthan*). In the organic body each part constantly maintains the whole, and is in maintaining the whole thereby itself maintained; just so stands the citizen in relation to the State.[1]

The attempt to give place to both artificial and organismic conceptions in the interpretation of the State is seen also in the writings of Heinrich Leo. In his *Natural Philosophy of the State*, 1833,[2] and his *Text-book of Universal History*, 1839-44,[3] he represents the State as natural and necessary in origin, and yet recognizes that in the later stages of State development elements appear that are consciously introduced by man, and that bear no organic relation either to one another or to the elements which are evolving naturally. Where these artificial elements are fundamental or permanent the State is mechanical, as distinguished from the higher, organic, State.

The State is natural in its origin, "directly given with mankind."[4] Wherever there are men their mutual relations are partially determined by the natural differentiations between leaders and followers, the strong and the weak, the ruling and the ruled. Direction and command, regulation and restraint, are exercised over the conduct of the individual by the more powerful or more competent one, several, or total group. "All social life begins with the State,"[5] which is the synthesis and embodiment of these natural political relations. The State is not something discovered by or for the nation, but is "an emanation from the inborn national spirit."[6] It has its

---

[1] *Grundlage*, p. 209.

[2] *Studien und Skizzen zu einer Naturlehre der Staates.*

[3] *Lehrbuch der Universalgeschichte*, 6 vols.

[4] *Naturlehre*, pp. 1-2.   [5] *Ibid.*, p. 3.   [6] *Ibid.*, p. 1.

own nature and law; and the political relations of the individuals of the State are bound up with, and modified by, their other natural characteristics. Thus the innermost spirit (*geistige Innigkeit*) of the nation, manifesting itself in the State-whole as well as in the members of the State, forms a limit which, at all stages of political development, the artificially transforming agencies inevitably encounter.[1]

Though in its unconscious origin and in the maturing relations of human society the State bears a natural and necessary character, yet there may come conditions under which men are compelled, in the exercise of conscious discretion and volition, to impose upon the State certain artificial features.[2] Such conditions may arise, in the first place, as the result of one-sided national development, which creates an inorganic heterogeneity; that is, where the principle of political formations is a single pursuit—such as the cultivation of the soil—or a single relation—such as the superior mental or physical power of a group in the nation—or a single idea—such as the fear of life after death. The division of the people on the basis of one of these principles is inorganic, maintained through force. In other words, the people are held apart in *castes*, instead of naturally distributing themselves into classes mutually supplementing each other according to their peculiar capabilities and motives. Thus, in a people wholly devoted to agriculture we find the groups of noble freemen and peasant serfs externally united by force.

In the second place, such a condition arises in the case of the subjection of one State by another and the conse-

---

[1] *Naturlehre*, p. 3.

[2] *Universalgeschichte*, vol. i, pp. 11 *et seq.*

quent bringing together of heterogeneous national types. If the conquered State is of widely different civilization and political genius from the conquering State, the latter can neither leave undisturbed the pre-existing political relations of the former nor implant within it its own political relations. The new composite State thus formed must bear the stamp of conscious human agency; it no longer possesses the character of having sprung from the *geistige Innigkeit des Volkes.*[1]

But even in such cases of necessarily artificial development, as in all efforts on the part of men to fix from without the State-structure, the nature both of man and of the State puts limits upon the influence of human agency. When a German people adopts the law and constitution of the French State, the character of these French institutions inevitably becomes modified by the peculiar genius of the German people. On the other hand,

the State itself is a spiritual whole, which like the spirit of the individual, has its own indwelling law; and all attempts to construct something arbitrary to occupy the place of the true State, and to set at nought the laws of its inner organization (*Gestaltung*), will fail. The general nature of the State is thus as firm a limit to human arbitrariness as is the nature of the individuals: and the truly divine power and elevation of the State appears in this—that the exertions of individuals to deform it can never reach its innermost essence.[2]

Leo explains that a distinction between "organic" and "mechanical" States may be made on the basis of the parts which the national State-life, on the one hand, and external force, on the other hand, respectively play

[1] *Op. cit.*, p. 12.   [2] *Ibid.*, p. 11.

in holding the members of the State together and in determining its development.[1]   A State in which the existence side by side of unassimilable racial or political elements, or the condition of one-sided industrial or cultural development, has made necessary a union and organization held together by force, is mechanical.   The individuals forming such a State are not inwardly joined to each other by the State but are merely externally and mechanically united.   A State which has not this character of forced union, but proceeds from the peculiarity of an independent natural social group, is organic.   "The rule of the mechanical State is given by a special interest—an interest either naturally more potent, or regarded as more important by the naturally more powerful members of the State; and the whole organization conforms to this interest through outer force.   The rule of life of the organic State proceeds naturally from the collective life of its members."[2]

4. METAPHYSICAL CONCEPTIONS OF ORGANISM

In the argument of Fichte and Leo we thus find organic principles in combination with artificial principles.   In Fichte's interpretation the State has a contractual basis; but the relation of the citizens to one another and to the State are explained in terms of organic interdependence.   The primary idea in Leo's interpretation is that of the natural origin and normally organic development of the State; man's conscious interference in political evolution is understood as only a modifying and contingent influence.

But the progress of the organismic ideas, as set forth by Herder, is more clearly and consistently traceable through

---

[1] *Naturlehre*, pp. 4 *et seq*.   [2] *Ibid*., pp. 4–5.

the political speculation of Schelling and Hegel; where, too, the transition from eighteenth-century political conceptions to the later theories of the State appears in a more logical form. With these philosophers the State is a product of will or of reason, but in the absolute and metaphysical sense that the State has the two essentially organic attributes of being an "end-in-itself" and of being "harmonized organically"—its components inevitably interconnected. Schelling regarded the State as a creation of the general will of the world soul; as the manifestation of the absolute in a harmony of necessity and freedom. Hegel took a step further in the organismic direction, conceiving the State as the development of the Idea into objective reality—the different phases of the manifestation constituting the different powers of the State, which must co-operate organically if the State is to survive. Among later writers—devoted more immediately to political theory—this metaphysical conception of the organic nature of the State is developed with more or less concrete sociological—or anthropological, and constitutional, relations. This appears in the "harmonic-organic" State of Krause and Ahrens, and the "ethical organism" of Schmitthenner and others.

(a) *The State-organism of Hegel and Schelling.*

Schelling gave comparatively little consideration to any phase of political theory. But his application of his general philosophy of nature to the State in his *Study of History and Jurisprudence* (1802)[1] evidently furnished the inspiration of some later theorists, whose writings were dominated by a form of the organismic conception the philosophical basis for which is to be found in his

[1] "Über das studium der Historie und der Jurisprudenz": the tenth number of his *Vorlesungen über die Methode des academischen Studiums.*

lecture. This presents the State as the creation of the general will; not, however, of the will of all, or a majority, of the members of the State, or of an average or general will—in any other sense—of the citizens; it is the creation of the will of the world soul.[1] The absolute manifests itself in nature and in man—its perfect manifestation is attained only in a harmony of necessity and freedom, of the general and the particular; the outer, real, form of this harmony is the State.

The State is thus the most exalted product of divine-human history; it is "the completed (*vollendete*) world of history," "the outer organism of a harmony—first reached in freedom itself—of necessity and freedom."[2] For this harmony has distinct forms according as it is expressed in the real or the ideal: the ideal form is the Church; the real, the State. "The perfect manifestation" (*vollkommende Erscheinung*) of the harmony in the real "is the perfect State, whose Idea is attained when the particular and the general are absolutely one; and when everything happening necessarily is at the same time free and everything happening freely is at the same time necessary."[3] The State, therefore, cannot be correctly explained as a means to any end, whatever that end may be—whether the general happiness, the satisfaction of the social impulses of men, or the greatest possible freedom in social life. The State must always be understood in its relation to the absolute. "A true interpretation . . . is not of the State as such, but of the absolute organism in the form of the State."[4] As "the direct and visible image of the absolute life," it cannot be considered as "the possibility of something else."[5] In

---

[1] *Cf.* Bluntschli, *Geschichte der neueren Staatswissenschaft*, p. 598.

[2] *Vorlesungen*, p. 214.   [3] *Ibid.*, p. 229.   [4] *Ibid.*, p. 235.   [5] *Ibid.*, p. 236.

fact, it will itself fulfill all ends, because it is the manifestation of the absolute.

The influence of Schelling's philosophical conception of the organic State appears in Hegel's idea of the State as the rationally organized expression of the general will. He founds the State on will and acknowledges Rousseau's service in having established that as the principle of the State.[1] But this principle with Hegel means a very different thing from the "general will" of Rousseau. He thus points out as the defect of Rousseau's philosophy that it recognized only concrete individual wills, consciously and arbitrarily entertained and expressed; it therefore conceived the general will only as the common element of the known individual wills. The general will of Hegel is something absolute, independent of subjective individual wills. It is the will of the World-spirit (*Weltgeist*); it is the rational (*Vernunftige*) in last abstraction. With Rousseau the union of individuals in the State is in the form of a contract based on their choice, conscious intent, optional and expressed sanction. To this Hegel opposes, as the principle of the State, the objective will—the "*rational in its concept*, whether or not apprehended (*erkannt*) by the individuals or willed by their desire (*Belieben*)."[2]

The State is defined as the "reality (*Wirklichkeit*) of the moral idea—of the moral spirit (*Geist*) . . . which thinks and knows itself and performs that which it knows in so far as it knows it."[3] The principle of the

---

[1] *Grundlinien der Philosophie des Rechts* (1820), p. 314.

[2] *Ibid.*, pp. 307–08. Bosanquet (*Philosophical Theory of the State*, p. 261) expresses Hegel's idea as follows: "The State is an imperative necessity of man's nature as rational, while contract is a mere agreement of certain free persons about certain external things."

[3] *Philosophie des Rechts*, p. 305.

unity of the State is thus essentially that of organic unity, namely, that of being absolutely its own end. The State thus has the "highest right (*Recht*) against the individuals, whose highest duty it is to be members of the State."[1]

Again: The State is the entrance (*Gang*) of God into the world; its foundation is the power of reason realizing itself as will. Absolute Reason—that is, God—realizes itself in the State.[2] Through the first—that is, logically first—stage in this unfolding of the idea of the state into immediate reality (*unmittelbare Wirklichkeit*) there is evolved the individual State as an organism (*als sich auf sich beziehender Organismus*).[3] The organism of the State is "the development of the idea into its distinctions and their objective reality"[4] in the political constitution (as distinguished from the other two logical stages of this manifestation of the State idea, *i. e.*, in "outer State-law"—the relation of the individual State to other States, and in "world history"—the final realization of the "world-soul").[5]

The constitution is thus the organization of a particular State in relation to itself. From the manifestation of the different elements of the State idea are developed the different powers (*verschiedene Gewalten*) in the constitution. The rationality of the State shows itself in the fact that it—the State—determines its activity according to the nature of its conception, and distinguishes itself into working powers each of which forms an individual whole. We thus have the legislative power, which determines and establishes the general; the government (*Regierung*), which subsumes particular spheres of ac-

[1] *Philosophie des Rechts*, p. 306.   [2] *Ibid.*, p. 313.
[3] *Ibid.*   [4] *Ibid.*, p. 325.   [5] *Ibid.*, pp. 313-14.

tion and individual cases under the general; and the princely power, which exercises the final decision as a subjectivity, and in which the different powers are comprehended into a unity.[1] According to the nature of an organism these powers must work together organically; if they fall apart or work independently of one another, the whole State falls into dissolution; it is like "the fable of the stomach and the other organs."[2]

(b) *The Harmonic-Organic State*

With Krause,[3] who was a contemporary and disciple of Schelling, the ideal State is the *Menschheitsstaat;* it is a "humanity-state" in that it would comprise all nations and States of the earth, and in that in it all the highest life purposes of mankind—religion, morality, science, art—would be striven for with regard for their "organic" interrelations. This "humanity-state" is to be regarded as completely realized only when, first, each nation (*Volk*) is organized into a State which combines in itself all lesser State persons (the present States, or other corporate communities, within a nation), each of the latter fitting in organically with the national organization; and when, secondly, these national States—each thus organically complete in itself—stand in organic constitutional interaction (*organischer Wechselwirkung des Rechtsleben*) and are all incorporated into the organic

---

[1] *Philosophie des Rechts*, p. 348.

[2] *Ibid.*, p. 324. For a suggestive interpretation of Hegel's theory, *cf.* Bosanquet, *op. cit.*, ch. x.

[3] *Cf.* especially his *System der Rechts-philosophie*, pp. 526 *et seq.;* and his *Abriss des Systems der Philosophie des Rechts oder des Naturrechts* (1828), *passim.* The former work is a posthumous publication (1874, edited by Röder) of his lectures at Berlin and Göttingen. *Cf.* also Bluntschli und Brater, *Deutsches Staatswörterbuch, loc. cit.*

union which constitutes the "humanity-state." The law of each subordinate State will be organically determined because, though it originates in the nature of that State, yet the latter must recognize and accept higher constitutional laws from all States above it. Further, in this ideal universal State, each side of human destiny would receive its due recognition, each component State would be allowed to fulfil its particular destiny and play its part in the co-operative attainment of the ends of humanity. The "humanity-state" is thus organic in these general respects of interrelation and co-operation of parts, the total activity being naturally apportioned and organized. Krause makes no very specific analysis of organic elements and functions and does not give much attention to the attributes of vitality and growth.

The general idea of Krause was elaborated, made more concrete, and added to, by his pupil and follower Heinrich Ahrens. This development is to be found chiefly in the latter's *Philosophy of Law* [1] (1837), particularly in the sections on *Der Cultur- oder Humanitäts-rechtsstaat.* Here also the determining idea is that of a harmonious development of humanity through a State in which the component communities and cultural organs co-operate in a common movement, each being allowed to fulfill its peculiar mission in that common purpose. However, the author's viewpoint is kept somewhat nearer to contemporary conditions, and the national-State idea is dominant. He says:

The constitutional State must be a true reflection of the or-

---

[1] *Naturrecht oder Philosophie des Rechtes und des Staats auf dem Grunde des ethischen Zusammenhangens von Recht und Cultur.* References here are to the sixth edition, 1870–71.

ganic character of the living national order (*Volksordnung*)
in which the freedom of all members and forces in self-govern-
ment forms the primary element, while the State-power exercises only guidance and over-sight; through co-operation of
all members and forces an organic interaction is established.
The great life-stream of the nation does not have its origin in
the State and public authority, but is formed by many springs
that flow forth in the local circles of communities, churches,
and provinces and in the various cultural groups; the outlets
of these springs must be confined within their proper chan-
nels and united by the State into a great, well-ordered current
which will divide itself again into many copious side-streams.[1]

In his *Organismic Theory of the State*[2] (1850), where
his conception is more specifically organismic, the State is
regarded as society in so far as it acts consciously through
a central directive power, and in so far as it is organized
for such consciously enforced social action.   The State
is the *Machtssphäre* of social *Willensthätigkeit*.[3]   In its
principal manifestations, he says, " the State is like the
nervous apparatus of the conscious will in connection
with the organs of animal motion subject to it."   But
in the animal organism the movement "is not throughout animal movement, but for the most part unconscious
reflex-movement, accomplished through the subordinate
spinal and sympathetic nerve-centres."   It is not otherwise in the social body: "Only a part of the total activity
of society comes within the sphere of force (*Machtssphäre*)—*i. e.* the State."   At the same time the idea
of the *Humanitätsrecht* is still fundamental.   For Ahrens
states it as one of the essentials of this *organische
Staatslehre*, that it conceives the State as a " social organ

[1] *Op. cit.*, sec. 116.   [2] *Organische Staatslehre.*
[3] *Ibid.*, pp. 23 *et seq.*

of humanity." [1] The State must always be considered in its relations to the physical, intellectual, moral, religious, and artistic activities and ends. It, though not embracing the whole of society, nor concentrating in itself all social activity, must always establish itself in harmony with religion, morality, science, and art, must derive from them support in its peculiar task, and render to them the aid that it is specially fitted to give.

In the detailed discussion, in the *Organische Staatslehre*, of the specific resemblances and differences between social and organic bodies, [2] biological analogy and terminology are freely applied, and the organic conceptions of physical science are made use of in the analysis of the organs and functions of the State. The differences are all explained by the fundamental distinction that there is manifest a knowing, valuing, and selective activity in determining the inner life and development of society, and that society deals with ideal goods to which there are no counterparts in the environment of the organic world proper. The human body is the last stage of organic development as such. The organic realm " does not ascend to still higher formations of a distinctly organic sort." [3]

As defined by the author, the central idea of the *Organische Staatslehre* is that it " conceives the State as an organism of society animated by its own peculiar idea, and [conceives] all its functions and relations in their organic connection and interaction." [4] However, he insists that the State is not a natural organism, and he would have his conception clearly distinguished from those organismic theories which attempt to carry over bodily the principles and categories of the natural

---

[1] *Organische Staatslehre*, p. 10.   [2] *Ibid.*, sec. iv.

[3] *Ibid.*, p. 18.   [4] *Ibid.*, p. 6.

sciences into the field of law and politics, and to interpret all the elements of the State as natural products.
A fundamental concept in Ahrens' theory is the element
of rational freedom in the nature and development of the
State. The State is essentially composed of men; the
attribute distinguishing men from all other terrestrial
beings is reason; the characteristic expression of reason
is in free action. Everywhere in the life of the State
appear the products of the activities of human freedom
in pursuit of rational ends of humanity; and this agency
becomes increasingly determining in the more developed
life of the State. "The State must, therefore, be a free
organism, in which the natural organic development, advancing in continuity, is harmoniously united with the
rational activity, independently self-determining according to conscious ends (*Zweckbegriffen*)." This theory
thus combines the subjective (*individuelle*) and the objective element of the State-life.[1] The living basis of the
State is the human personality with its own sphere of
action and its rights. As indicated above, a source and
factor in every phase and stage of the State-life is to be
found within the life of the individual man. "But, on
the other side, there must also be recognized the *organic*
or *social* (*gemeinschaftliche*) element, which is given in
the *objective* concept of law and State." This is "the
principle of co-ordinating unity, . . . of limitation of
the legal and political activity of the individuals, so
that the individual in his private and public spheres of
right, in subordination to a principle equally dominating
all, becomes a part of the whole in organic limitation
and interaction, and the right of the aggregate, as bearer
of the objective idea, becomes authoritative for the rights
of the individuals."[2]

[1] *Organische Staatslehre*, pp. 7–9.   [2] *Ibid.*, p. 9.

(c) *The Ethical Organism*

By several political metaphysicians of about the middle of the century the State is explained as an *ethical organism*. In this conception again the organic attribute is considered in a chiefly philosophical sense. The term organic is used to indicate, first, the character, possessed by the more permanent institutions among mankind, of having the ground and explanation of their existence in themselves; and, secondly, the natural and essentially interdependent relations of the elements of these institutions. The term ethical is applied to these organic institutions in all cases where the active members of them are beings endowed with consciousness and free-will.

This conception appears in its most philosophical aspect in F. J. Schmitthenner's *Twelve Books Concerning the State* (1839), especially his *Principles of General Public Law* (1845).[1] His theory of the State is based on a Platonic doctrine of the "idea." He defines the organic as "the external manifestation of an objective spiritual principle . . . the emerging of the ideal into reality."[2] Everything that is subject to development has as its essence an "idea." The "idea" of anything is its destiny (*Bestimmung*)—its end; it is the spiritual prototype of that which is to be.[3] The "idea" of a thing determines its general nature and development, though the particular manifestations are variously conditioned by outward circumstances. The manifestations are diverse at different stages of development and under different associations with other manifestations, but there is a persistent movement towards a more complete realization

---

[1] The *Zwölf Bücher vom Staate* was never completed. Vols. i and iii were published, and the latter had the special title, *Grundlinien des allgemeinen oder idealen Staatsrechts.*

[2] *Grundlinien*, p. 20.   [3] *Ibid.*, p. 256.

of the idea. This is a necessary process; no human agency can permanently obstruct or derange it. "The idea must exist" (*Die Idee soll sein*); that is its characteristic attribute.[1]

In the realm of humanity this relation of "idea" and manifestation holds not only for individual persons, but also for associations of persons—the family, the church, the State. The State is necessary and organic. It has the ground of its being within itself—its "idea"; its "idea" is "the spiritual prototype of a system of institutions of law, culture, and material well-being, under which the nation (*Volk*) is to attain (*soll erstreben*) the destiny of mankind."[2] Man's existence in the State is necessary and his relation to it organic because "the State is a necessary postulate" for him; he "cannot attain his destiny outside of it."[3] For he is a fragment of society and of the nation. "Separated from his connection with this living whole he is a wholly inconceivable phenomenon; his finest feelings and forces—love, duty, language—belong not to the individual, but to the social life."[4] The State is "the organic system of public life, or the organic form of society, in which a nation strives to accomplish its destiny."[5]

The State is, furthermore, an "*ethical* organism." An entity is "ethical" if the realization of its "idea" is accomplished through the action of conscious will. "An idea is ethical in that, having its existence in the element (*im Elemente*) of consciousness, it is related to a free will."[6] An ethical organism is accordingly an organism

---

[1] *Grundlinien*, pp. 7, 258.   [2] *Ibid.*, p. 259.

[3] *Zwölf Bücher vom Staate*, vol. i, p. 23.

[4] *Grundlinien*, p. 254.   [5] *Ibid.*, p. 4.

[6] *Grundlinien*, p. 257.

in which particular functions are executed by members endowed with free-will.[1] The element of conscious free-will in the State is that of the individual members of the State. Man, besides having his own independent (*selbständigen*) destiny, enters as an element into the process of the development of the "idea" of the State; his *Aufgabe* is involved in the destiny of the nation—or other particular society—to which he belongs.[2]

The main body of Georg Waitz's *First Principles of Politics* (1862)[3] is devoted to questions of organization and administration, and to a detailed exposition of his view of the proper constitution of the State of his time. This delineation shows the influence of contemporary political facts in Germany and stands in no necessary logical relation to the introductory section on *The Nature of the State*, in which is briefly set forth the author's interpretation of the State as an ethical organism. Yet the author does make his own analysis accord with such ideas as that of the essential continuity in State development, of the constant causal correlation between State-form and the stage of general cultural development of the people, of the futility of attempts at abstract or arbitrary amelioration in the State organization. These ideas we usually find to follow a definition of the State as an organism.

Such a definition the author gives very briefly in the opening pages of the Introduction. Having affirmed that "the State is the institution for the realization of the moral life-ends of mankind, in so far as this [realization] takes place in associated life in nations (*in dem Zusammenleben nach Völkern erfolgt*)," he goes on to

---

[1] *Zwölf Bücher vom Staate*, vol. i, sec. 3.

[2] *Grundlinien*, p. 257.   [3] *Grundzüge der Politik*.

say that "the State is nothing arbitrarily made and has not arisen through contract of men or through the might of one or several individuals"; "it grows up organically as an organism." The State is not, however, to be identified in concept with a natural organism; its laws and its ends are not those of "natural life"; it rests on the higher moral capacities of man; in it moral ideas govern; it is no natural, but an ethical organism.[1]

In this idea of the State as an ethical organism Waitz seeks to harmonize the elements of freedom and necessity. Though the State is "given with mankind, necessary, and of eternal duration,"[2] yet in the course of its evolution it is subject to man's freely manifested predisposition to development. Though its own laws set a limit to the extent of man's influence over its evolution, yet within these limits the particular form in which the State appears with a given people is determined by the free conduct of that people. "As in history in general, so also in the history of States, necessity and freedom go together; the nation can fashion its *Staatsform* thus or otherwise, as an individual man may for a period potently interfere with the course of State development; over all, however, reigns a law (*Gesetz*) of development."[3] In conformity to the definition of the State as the institution for the realization, according to nations, of the moral life-ends of mankind, the character of the State must vary according as these life-tasks are differently conceived by different nations; and these are differently conceived according to differences in national character and in development.

The State, as an organism, receives its law (*Recht*)— that is, its system of organization (*Ordnung*)—not from

---

[1] *Grundzüge*, p. 5.   [2] *Ibid.*, p. 6.   [3] *Ibid.*, p. 8.

without, but from within.[1]   Therefore, the constitution
(*Verfassung*)—the formulation of the law of the State—
"should contain nothing which has not issued from, and
does not live in, the consciousness of the nation ; . . . it
should not be subjected to frequent alteration, nor regarded as something accidental and arbitrary."[2]   Furthermore, the end of the State—as an organism—is in
itself.   The State cannot be said to exist for the attainment of some ulterior motive : such as the well-being or
happiness of the people, or the fostering of their bodily
or spiritual possessions.   "Everything organic bears the
ground of its being in itself.   The State is its own end
(*Der Staat ist sich selbst Zweck*)." [3]

[1] *Grundzüge*, p. 9.   [2] *Ibid.*, pp. 9–10.   [3] *Ibid.*, p. 11.

Supplementary Note.—The theory of the ethical-organic State is held
in some form by other thinkers also.

Cf. Franz Vorländer, " Die Staatsformen in ihrem Verhältnis zu der
Entwicklung der Gesellschaft," *Zeitschrift für die gesammte Staatswissenschaft*, vol. xv (1859), pp. 143–187.   "Wenn der Staat seinem
Begriff nach eine nothwendige, wesentliche, selbständige Richtung des
Lebens der Gesellschaft oder des Volks begründet, so wird dieses
politische Leben, wie alle Lebensformen, in einer Mannigfältigkeit
verschiedener Lebensrichtungen sich darstellen welche zusammen ein
lebendiges, zweckmässig geordnetes Ganzes, d. h. ein solches bilden,
worin die verschiedenen Lebensrichtungen in ihren verschiedenen
Funktionen und Bildungen sich gegenseitig ergänzen und die einzelnen
Bildungen zum Ganzen sich verhalten als Organe, d. h. nicht bloss als
äussere Werkzeuge und Mittel, sondern als vom Leben des Ganzen
durchdrungene Glieder, welche durch ihre Thätigkeiten nach verschiedenen Seiten hin die Bedürfnisse des Ganzen zweckmässig befried-
igen" (p. 150).   "Der Staat hat zugleich eine selbstbewusste sittliche
Existenz in den Seelen der Menschen und eine natürliche in den Or-
ganen der Macht.   Wenn in der neuesten Zeit der Staat als ein ethischer
Organismus bezeichnet worden ist, so bezeichnet dieser Begriff seinen
Unterschied von den Natur-organismen; derselbe darf aber nicht mit
dem des Sittlichen identificirt, sondern muss in antiken Sinne aufge-
fasst werden, wonach der Staat aus dem Ethos des Volks hervorgeht"
(pp. 151–2).

Cf. F. A. Trendelenburg, *Naturrecht auf dem Grunde der Ethik*

The theories that we have so far considered represent
the State as organic only in a general and abstract way.
None of them attempts to classify the State within the
realm of physical organisms, or to draw any very close
or detailed parallelism between its structure and functions and the structure and functions of plant and animal
life. With many writers of the nineteenth century, however, the organismic idea took a more concrete and positive form. The completeness or detailed extent to which
this idea is followed out differs with the different individuals of this general group of writers, as will appear.

(1860), especially secs. 18–19, 40–41, 150–1. Trendelenburg distinguishes
ethical organisms from organisms of nature as follows : " Es ist der
Charakter des organischen Ganzen, dass seine Idee vor den Theilen ist
und die Theile für die Zwecke seines Lebens ausbildet und dass nicht
umgekehrt die Theile, vor der Gemeinschaft selbständig, das Ganze aus
ihrer Macht zusammensetzen. Denselben über die Theile übergreif-
enden Charakter hat die ethische Gemeinschaft, wenn sie z. B. für die
Regierung, für die Rechtspflege, für die Vertheidigung Einrichtungen
schafft, welche ohne sie keinen Bestand haben, auf ähnliche Weise, wie
Hand and Fuss, Auge und Ohr, als Theile besondere Zwecke des
Lebens ausführend, vom Leibe losgelöst, vergehen. Aber der Unterschied beider Arten von Organismen liegt in den letzten Elementen.
In den Organismen der Natur schieden sie aus dem Organischen ins
Chemische und gehen in die ungestaltete Natur, in die Masse zurück.
Aber die letzen Elemente des ethischen Ganzen sind Individuen, nicht
selbstlos wie die Theile eines belebten Wesens in der Natur, sondern in
eigenem Mittelpunkt gegründet, dergestallt dem Ganzen in der Idee
ebenbürtig, dass es zweifelhaft sein kann, ob das Individuum am
Ganzen, oder das Ganze am Individuum sein Vorbild hat. Das Ganze
ist Gesellschaftsbildung, eine Vereinsbildung höherer Ordnung, als die
Naturwissenschaft in dem aus Individuen von Sprossen oder Zellen
geeinigten Bau der Pflanzen und Thiere annimmt." *Ibid.*, p. 59.

Cf. Joseph Held, *Staat und Gesellschaft vom Standpunkte der
Geschichte der Menschheit und des Staats* (1861–5, 3 vols.), vol. i (pp.
575–597), Anhang II: "Ueber den Begriff des Organismus und seine
Anwendung auf die Gesellschaft." Held explains that the free and
ethical character of the members of society produces a distinction between the social-organism (or the State-organism, *cf. ibid.*, pp. 197

But they may be differentiated more logically by classifying them according to the particular phase of organic life which they predominantly or exclusively consider in their analysis of the State. Upon this basis are to be distinguished two prevailing tendencies, which we may call the *psychic* and the *biological*. With those theorists who follow the former tendency, reflections on the State are based primarily on the sentient or psychic aspects of higher organic life; while by those of the latter tendency the physical structure and vital processes of physical organisms are employed in the interpretation of the State.

et seq.) and natural beings. " Der menschliche Gesellschafts-organismus kann nie in dem Sinne ein volkommener sein, wie ein reiner Naturkörper als solcher nach dem Naturgesetze es ist. Die Ursache hiervon liegt in der Freiheit der den Gesellschafts-organismus bildenden Glieder. Die eben hieraus entstehende relative Unvollkommenheit des Gesellschafts-organismus ist der Grund der Unvermeidlichkeit mancher Störungen des rein organischen Ganzes seiner geschichtlichen Entwickelung, aber der Grund einer dem blossen Naturkörper fehlenden unendlichen Perfectibilität." *Ibid.*, pp. 579-580. "Die Verbindung der Glieder mit dem Organismus in der menschlichen Gesellschaft wesentlich eine sittliche, eine freie sein, d. h. sie muss von allen Gliedern, welches auch deren Stellung im Organismus sei, eben wegen ihrer gleichmässig-organischen Stellung gleichmässig, und nach Massgabe dieser Stellung verschieden angestrebt werden." *Ibid.*, p. 582. *Cf* also *ibid.*, vol. ii, pp. 498 *et seq.*, and vol. iii, pp. 676 *et seq.*

For further citations from the works of exponents of the ethical-organic and harmonic-organic theories, *cf.* Krieken, *op. cit.*, p. 108, note 3.

CHAPTER II

The Psychic Conception of the State

The political philosophy which considers the State in its human or psychological aspects may be logically regarded as forming a transition between the early nineteenth-century ideas of the State as organism in a metaphysical sense, and the theories—reaching their fuller development later—which treat the State as organic in the sense of natural science. In the treatises now to be examined the organismic idea is taken in a more concrete way than in any that we have so far studied. But still not organism in general, but particularly the human organism—or the sentient, rather than the physical side of the higher types of organic life—forms the basis of comparison.

By some the State is depicted as possessing all the fundamental attributes of human personality; by others it is compared with man primarily with respect to the "ages" of a human being. In the treatises following the latter method—which we will consider first because they appear earlier—the "ages" are regarded as also representing "types" according to which States, as well as individual men, may be psychologically classified. Thus political development, either of a given State or in a general way, may be shown to pass through stages corresponding to the human life-periods—childhood, youth, etc.; or the treatise may have to do chiefly with the analysis of the different kinds of State as distinguished by psychological character, which depends upon degree of psychological development.

I. THE ORGANISMIC ANALOGIES OF GÖRRES

Before taking up the two schools characterized above, it seems worth while to devote some attention to an early example of anthropomorphic parallelization which can not be properly grouped with either of these schools, or with the later developing political *Naturlehre*. This example is to be found in the political essays of the brilliant writer, Joseph von Görres. In his *Germany and the Revolution* (1819),[1] he makes frequent recourse to the organic world in general for analogies and metaphors by means of which to make clear his argumentation or exhortation; but it is in the nature of the human organism in particular that the parallelisms are chiefly sought. This method is applied throughout the essay. It is sufficient for our purpose to consider a typical part and one in which the analogizing is more completely followed out and in which the treatment more nearly approaches logical form.

In this essay Görres compares the democratic and monarchic elements in the constitution of the State to the automatic and voluntary elements in the physiology and psychology of man. This comparison is applied to the characterization of the two corresponding classes of the national population and their attitude towards government; and to the distinction between the representative and the centralized components of the governmental or-

[1] *Teutschland und die Revolution*, in vol. iv, pp. 65–482, of his *Politische Schriften*, München, 1859–60. Other early nineteenth-century writers who liken various parts of the State-structure to faculties or organs of the human being are C. A. von Wangenheim, *Die Idee der Staatsverfassung* (1815), and C. A. Eschenmaier, *Normalrecht* (1819). See von Mohl, *Staatswissenschaften*, p. 257.

ganization, and to a determination of the relative part each should play. His conclusions form the basis of his interpretation of the past, present, and future politics of the German States.

The history of German States, he says, shows a continually recurring lack of adjustment between two opposing principles in the State-life, corresponding to two contrary elements in the individual organism. We find in the latter two sorts of activity, two systems of functions: the automatic and the voluntary.[1] These two systems exist together, but vary in relative importance at different times. Within the automatic sphere are to be classed the "natural," vegetative, and instinctive actions; these include the functions of the digestive, circulatory, and respiratory systems, as well as external reflex actions and also the involuntary train of thought and feelings. The voluntary element in the individual comprises the higher activities, which are only indirectly subject to the outer relations of nature and to the laws of fixed recurrence, and are controlled only by the self-conscious will—freely acting and self-determining.

Corresponding to the automatic and the voluntary elements in the individual organisms, we find in the State the democratic and the monarchic elements. As in the automatic sphere of the individual life the several activities follow their own particular laws, uncontrolled by the central will, so in a pure democracy the particularistic and automatic tendencies are seen in the effort of the most elementary parts of the national body—the individuals, families, minor associations—to keep themselves free from direction by a higher central power; there is aversion to authority and reliance upon self-support and

[1] *Op. cit.*, pp. 185 *et seq.*

self-guidance; we find thus the determination of all things from below upwards—in other words, popular government.

On the other hand, as in the voluntary part of individual life all activities are subject to a central will which from above controls and co-ordinates the separate movements, so in a pure monarchy this synthetic tendency is seen in the unquestioning obedience to a central higher power, the willing effacement of the individual in the community, the determination of everything from above downwards—in other words, autocratic government.

The order in which these two corresponding elements respectively preponderate is the same in the State as in the individual organism; the more democratic State organization precedes the more monarchic, as the more automatic life of the organism precedes the more voluntary. In the early German State the democratic element was pre-eminent until, through the unification by Charlemagne and the influence of the monarchically-organized Roman church, a State was evolved in which both principles were properly combined. When Charlemagne, "honoring the old principle of Germanic freedom and allowing every development from below upwards, artfully united that principle with the Christian monarchic principle of development from above downwards through the whole series of imperial officers, who in war and peace held their authority exclusively from the highest power, he formed the first truly organic world-state,"[1] resembling the complete man in his highest development. Then followed the dissolution of the empire soon after Charlemagne, the preponderance of the democratic element again, followed by excessive centralization in the

[1] *Op. cit.*, p. 191.

separate kingdoms in the opposition to democratic tendencies; and through these transformations may be traced
the varying ascendency of these two principles.

The condition of Germany at present, Görres holds,
is that of disorder resulting from the too great prevalence of the monarchic tendency. Its condition is like
that of somnambulism in an individual, when excessive
exercise of the higher central faculties produces in reaction mental torpidity and impotence of will, while the
lower organs become more active and the body moves
as in a sleep-wandering.[1] Following the recent over-
exertion of power and authority by the governing organs
of the State, a reaction is imminent, stirrings among the
third estate are beginning and the functions abandoned
by the now dormant sovereignty are being assumed by
the people. Proper adjustment will be regained by the
restoration of the organic harmony between the democratic and monarchic principles. The people must be
free and at the same time directed by the monarchy. In
the local communities internal affairs should be administered by elective officers, general affairs by officers
centrally appointed. In the intermediate stages the administrative magistracies of the districts and provinces
should be organized in such a way that the relative predominance of the democratic and monarchic principles
in these magistracies would vary with their respective
proximity to the people and the central government.

A. *THE PSYCHOLOGICAL AGES OF THE STATE*

2. WELCKER

Carl Theodor Welcker, in his *The Ultimate Grounds
of Law, State and Punishment* (1813),[2] was one of the

[1] *Op. cit.*, p. 196.
[2] *Die letzten Gründe von Recht, Staat, und Strafe.* Cf. especially
pp. 1-20.

earliest of the nineteenth-century political theorists to describe the "ages" (*Lebensalten*) of political development, comparing each with the corresponding life-period of an individual man, and to define the characteristics of a given State in accordance with the particular age through which it is passing. A nation and a State, he maintains, like individual man, have each a childhood, youth, manhood, and "old age." The character of the government of a State bears essential relation to the age of the nation, and the attributes of each age of the nation are those of the corresponding age of a human being.

In the infancy of a people, as in a man's childhood, sensuosity is the controlling principle of conduct and nature. The actuating motives in either case are selfish satisfaction of the senses, the avoidance of physical harm. In this age of a nation, therefore, the rule of the physically powerful prevails, and there arises what is called the "law of the stronger" (*Recht des Stärkeren*); but that is better designated as the "law of sense" (*Recht der Sinnlichkeit*), since on this foundation the stronger attains his mastery and the weaker, through fear, is reduced to obedience. In this condition the despotic State comes into existence: from the inevitable conflict of sensuous interests either the weaker are subdued through the cunning and power of the stronger, or all voluntarily—weary of the strife—subject themselves to the rule of a despot. The primitive State is accordingly a despotism.

The later types of State—theocracy, constitutional State, and despotism, likewise make their appearance in logical conformity to the character of the contemporary age of the nation. In the youth of a nation, as in that of the individual man, the determining attribute is that of an unreflecting trust in the agency of a controlling and protecting divinity; in a political way this manifests itself in the theocratic form and principles which the State assumes. With the development of reason in the nation's manhood comes a recognition and formulation of the rights of individuals and of the ends of the State and an intelligent institution of the means whereby these are protected or secured; in other words, in this rational age of the nation the constitutional State appears. Finally, with the perversion of the faculties of reason and religious emotion, marking the inevitable decay of old age, the State relapses into its primitive despotic form—a despotism in which, however, superior subtlety, rather than superior physical power, constitutes the basis of the selfish rule of the stronger over the weaker.

3. ROHMER

Nowhere has a physiological interpretation of the State-life been more thoroughly and distinctively set forth than in the *Theory of Political Parties* (1844) of Friedrich and Theodor Rohmer.[1] The theory is an attempt to characterize and explain, through an application of the results of Friedrich Rohmer's former psychological studies, political parties—those of the present as well as those of history—and to pass judgment upon them and determine the relative authority proper to each of them.

The most significant features of the psychological studies are:[2] the conception of the "basal forces" (*Grundkräfte*) of the human soul; the laws of their development in the four life-stages; the application of these

---

[1] *Friedrich Rohmers Lehre von den politischen Parteien.* The author of this work is Theodor Rohmer, who published it after the death of his elder brother, Friedrich. References here are to the edition of 1885.

[2] *Cf.* Bluntschli und Brater, *Staatswörterbuch*, viii, pp. 645 *et seq.*

laws to an interpretation of the history of mankind; and
the determination through these laws of the distinctions
of individual character and of the highest types of humanity. The human soul is analyzed as a perfectly articulated organism of sixteen basal forces; the eight forces
of the mind (*Geisterkräften*) have their seat in the head,
the eight forces of the heart (*Gemütskräften*) in the
body; in each group half are active and half are passive;
again, half are directed outwards and half inwards. The
successive supremacy of these different forces governs
the life-course of the soul organism as a whole—and,
therefore, the development of the body also, as the body
is the product of the soul. In childhood and old age the
passive and receptive mental and spiritual forces prevail,
in youth and manhood the creative and conserving forces
are dominant. In the two former periods the proper
attitude of man is one of submission and obedience; in
the two latter, his normal position is that of authority
and command.[1]

The workings of these life-stages in the national psychology is the subject of the *Theory of Political Parties*.
The logical foundation and justification of the psychological method of the study of the State is distinctly
stated in the introductory chapters. "The highest
manifestation of the human mind in this life is the State."
Therefore, the State must be contained in the human
mind; its grounds and its form (*Ordnung*) must be
sought in the structure and faculties of the individual
mind. "In the organism of the human soul lies the
whole organism of the State. From the elements and
laws of the human soul the State has developed with
necessity; everything which pertains to the State—con-

[1] *Cf.* Bluntschli, *Geschichte*, pp. 751-2.

sequently the political parties—can find only in the human soul their explanation and justification." [1]

The State as such can be thought of without political parties, just as the individual as such can be conceived without regard to his age. The parts of the State, its whole mechanism, the elements of its population, and the organization of its classes and institutions, can be described without consideration of the political parties. But the moment the State in movement—in growth and development—becomes the object of examination, the political parties in the State necessarily come into view. "In order to understand the State-body I must study the parts of the human soul; in order to comprehend the State-life, I must study the laws of development of the human soul." [2]

That the author applied his mind to the State-life and its development as recorded in the changing relations of political parties, rather than to the State-body at rest, is probably to be accounted for chiefly from the actual circumstances which led him into political speculation. The first expression of these reflections was delivered during the period of his sojourn at Zürich and of his participation in the lively contest of the liberal-conservative party against the radical and the absolutist movements. Partly to his party affiliation—though partly, at least indirectly, to his natural temperament also—is probably to be attributed the fervor with which he argues for the logical political preëminence of the conservative and liberal elements of the nation. [3]

As all men, Rohmer continues, however different in

[1] *Lehre von den politischen Parteien*, secs. 13, 14.
[2] *Ibid.*, secs. 15-17.
[3] *Cf.* Bluntschli and Brater, *Staatswörterbuch*, viii, p. 648.

individual attributes, pass essentially through the same general development, so States, whatever their character may be, are subject to the same general evolution through the parties.[1] "The origin of parties proceeds from the organic development of men, that is, from the life-stages of the human mind. These life-stages are manifested in the ages. The development itself, as it is unfolded in the succession of the different stages, is history. The stages, however, as independent phenomena (*selbständige Gestaltungen*) and existing contemporaneously, are the *parties*."[2]

The basis, thus, for the description and distinction of political parties is in the life-ages of man : namely, boyhood, youth, full manhood (*der bestandene Mann*), and old age.[3] Though each man passes through these four stages, the distinctions between the ages are primarily relative ; each boy is radical as compared with what he will be when older ; each man, however radical his general character may be, is more conservative in his maturity than in the other stages of his life.[4] Some men, comparatively speaking, are in the old age stage all through life ; some, similarly, are always "youthful." Alcibiades was from birth a boy ; Pericles, a youth ; Caesar, a mature man ; Augustus, an old man. Corresponding to these four ages there are the four types of political parties: radicalism, liberalism, conservatism, and absolutism,[5] Rohmer seeks to determine the political place and function of each party through a joint examination of the characteristics of it and the age to which it corresponds. The analysis in each case is under five

---

[1] *Lehre von den politischen Parteien*, sec. 18.
[2] *Ibid.*, secs. 19–21.   [3] *Ibid.*, secs. 22 *et seq.*
[4] *Ibid.*, secs. 33 *et seq.*   [5] *Ibid.*, sec. 38.

heads, namely, general nature, intellectual quality, moral temperament, cosmic and religious view, and political doctrine.

In the boyhood of a man and in the radical party of the State[1] we find excessive mobility—aversion to repose, a constant desire for innovation for the mere sake of change. Their natural vigor shows itself in opposition; they are impatient of all restraints upon the following of their impulses; the radical party is normally the party of opposition. From lack of experience their actions show lack of practicality; radicalism seeks to extirpate by decree institutions whose roots stand deep in the history and sentiment of the nation. They seek to supply deficiency in experience through acquisition of knowledge; radicalism advocates universal education as a panacea. Intellectually, boyhood and radicalism are characterized by talent, rather than by insight or sagacity. As the boy lives in his world of dreams and phantasies, so intellectual radicalism busies itself with fanciful ideas of freedom, equality, universal brotherhood and peace, without concerning itself as to the possibility or the method of realization. Their understanding is formal, abstract, and mathematical. In their reckless disregard of danger, their ready sensibility to wrong and injustice, their quick vision and enthusiastic action, they may often, in circumstances where greater deliberation and circumspection might result fatally, prove themselves agencies for good. But these same qualities make them elements of disorganization and obstruction, if they endeavor to take the lead in the normal course of life; and the same emotional susceptibility that makes them excessively tender at one time may incite them to acts of

[1] *Op. cit.*, secs. 44–91.

barbaric cruelty at another. The boy and the radical man can see in the universe only abstract unity or physical plurality, with no harmonizing principle. In philosophical attitude they are thus either mystics or sophists, in religion either fanatics or sceptics. In politics, finally, as a result of limited and undeveloped intelligence—making possible only an abstract and mechanical view of things—radicalism desires, above everything else, equality. Like the boy the radical man is more eager for equality than for freedom; while he desires to do what is pleasing to himself, he is even more ardent that no one of his fellows should be more highly privileged than himself. He prefers a despotism to an aristocracy or to any constitution which recognizes the existence of classes. His political ideal is the equalization of all rights and of culture, the abrogation of all distinctions of nationality, unlimited freedom of trade, the leveling of all classes. The fundamental character of radicalism may thus be designated as "the abasement of organic life under the unlimited omnipotence of abstraction" (*die Beugung des organischen Lebens unter die unumschränkte Allmacht der Abstraktion*).[1]

The young man and liberalism represent man and the nation in the prime of their respective lives.[2] Their general characteristics are: an attitude of unhampered but friendly criticism and inquiry toward the world, tolerance and impartiality in their judgments of it; fullness of intellectual and physical strength; a creative and organizing genius—in knowledge and the arts, in church and State. Their distinguishing intellectual attribute is genius—genius in discerning (*erkennen*) where talent learns, in creating where talent fancies, in thinking where talent

---

[1] *Op. cit.*, p. 132.   [2] *Ibid.*, secs. 92–146.

dreams. Their philosophy is natural and rational, not formal and scholastic; they apply psychological, instead of mathematical and mechanical, standards in their classification of men; they unite thought and action, theory and practice, rooting their ideals in ideas. Though the eyes of liberalism, like those of the young man, are turned towards the future, it recognizes that historical institutions have their basis in human nature, and so cannot be eradicated until others are established to take their place. Instead of the vanity and self-assertion of radicalism and boyhood, liberalism and the young man have calm pride and a strong sense of justice. Liberalism and the young man see in the universe subordination and superordination, not co-ordination alone. To men they attribute relative freedom or dependence according to the "gradation of forces given them by God." They regard humanity as a great collective individual in the aggregate life of which each member has rights and duties appropriate to the position in which he finds himself by nature. Liberalism, finally, regards the State also as an organism, as therefore impossible of being formed by any kind of human contract; an aggregate organism, nevertheless, in which the organic position of the individuals does not necessarily remain fixed from one generation to the next, nor prevent the son of a peasant from rising to the nobility; for that position is determined by virtue and intellect, not by external relations, education, and training. We may, then, name this as the fundamental character of liberalism: " the domination of individuality, with respect both to the individuals and to the aggregate." [1]

The distinctive capacity of full manhood and of conserv-

[1] *Op. cit.*, pp. 223–4.

atism is for maintaining, organizing and improving that which has already been created or acquired.[1] Their pre-disposition is aversion to any change unless they see therein a distinct betterment of the present, and willingness to restore what of past good has been abandoned without sufficient reason. The breadth of their experience and the solidarity of their intellectual and cultural beliefs and purposes make them peculiarly fit to rule. Intellectually they are characterized by wisdom, which is less productive than genius but more discriminating, less penetrating but more comprehensive. Pre-eminent in sagacity and strength of memory, their habit of mind is to apply the historical, rather than the psychological, standard of judgment. Conservatism and full manhood are the stages in which practical efficiency reaches its highest development; to neither dogmas (as with the radicals) nor principles (as with the liberals) are the positive demands of actual life sacrificed. The conservative and the mature man are led to their religious tenets primarily through experience, rather than through speculation or insight. They perceive order as well as freedom in the world. The principle of freedom is that each should attain the highest of which he is capable; the principle of order is that no one should strive for a higher goal than is proper for him. Where liberalism emphasizes individuality almost exclusively, conservatism regards the claims and benefits of social and blood heredity and recognizes the efficacy of tradition. Finally, in their political aspect they stand for the sovereignty of families (*Geschlechter*) rather than of persons; for the power of tradition primarily, of the idea, only secondarily. Their political excellence is moderation,

---

[1] *Op. cit.*, secs. 150–177.

more than virtue; their interest is in private more than in public law, and in private more than in political freedom. The fundamental character of conservatism is the "domination of traditional right, achieved through inherited status and possession."[1]

The party of absolutism—similar to the old age of man—represents the completion of experience and the fixity and unchangeableness of opinions, which have become a part of its nature.[2] Its consequent repugnance to all change and its exalted idea of its own position as the end of all experience make it the party of intolerance and despotism. The intellectual peculiarity of the old man and of absolutism lies in their faculty of giving finish and symmetry to the sum of knowledge acquired. This faculty is coldly analytical and formal, and leads to mere abstraction or mere physical combination; its theories are mechanical or merely empirical; it emphasizes the forms and letters of laws and customs. In morals they are marked by lassitude and whimsicalness, and their virtue needs constantly the support of conventions and maxims. In things of religious belief old age and absolutism know only blind subservience or complete disorder, literal orthodoxy or atheism. Finally, as the abstract reasoning of the old man leads him to consider the State as divinely or arbitrarily constituted, so the absolutist's State is either a " divine-right " monarchy, or a State founded on an artificial contract which instituted either an absolute monarchy (as with Hobbes) or an absolute popular sovereignty (as with Rousseau). The inherent moral and intellectual infirmity of the absolutist party renders its political supremacy always precarious; it is therefore led to extreme formalism in

[1] *Op. cit.*, p. 278.   [2] *Ibid.*, secs. 178–204.

administration and to a strict application of the legiti-
macy doctrine.   Its State-structure is thus highly artificial, and money and birth, even after they have lost all
connection with hereditary ability and sentiment remain
its chief criteria of political gradation.   Absolutism thus
denotes everywhere the domination of form.[1]

It should be understood that the theory just outlined
as a theory of the basal types of political party corresponding to basal types of individual mind and character, does not imply, to the author, the existence of all
or any of these parties in any given nation at a given
epoch.   The types exist where no corresponding actual
political parties exist; there are always conservative,
radical, liberal, and absolutist individuals.   At the same
time Rohmer believes that the great parties of history
readily lend themselves to this classification.   For example: as radicals are to be classified the English Radicals and the French Revolutionists; as liberals, the
Plebeians of Rome, the Whigs of England, and the followers of Luther in the Reformation movement; as con-
servatives, the Roman Patricians and the English Tories;
as absolutists, the Spanish Carlists and the French Mon-
archists of the eighteenth century.[2]

The leadership and government of the State pertain
properly and naturally to the liberal and conservative
elements; to the former when the State-life demands
chiefly initiatory, institutive, reformative activities; to
the latter when conservation, organization, and reclama-
tion, or restoration, are the functions primarily essential.[3]   Though radicalism, or absolutism, may safely attain
a provisional authority in times when an evil resulting

---

[1] *Op. cit.*, secs. 203–04.   [2] *Ibid.*, sec. 41.
[3] *Ibid.*, secs. 100, 151 *et al.*

from an already existing preponderance of the one element can be removed only through the temporary sway of the other, in normal conditions their participation in political activity should be indirect, and subsidiary and supplementary to the controlling agency of the liberal and conservative elements.[1]

In the history of political organization four types of State constitutions may be distinguished according to these four political types of mankind:[2] radicalism produces the "Idol-State"; liberalism, the "Individual-State"; conservatism, the "Race-State"; and absolutism, the "Form-State." The nature of each constitution reveals its ideal basis and "the point of view upon which the authority of the sovereign rests."[3] The sanctity of the sovereign in the Idol-State is purely abstract, resting simply upon the office (in a monarchy) or upon the abstract conception of popular sovereignty (in a republic); the ideal of this State is an abstract doctrine—for example, equality and freedom. In the Individual-State the personality—that is, the character, accomplishments, mental endowment, *etc.*—of the sovereign is that to which respect is rendered; the ideal upon which this State is organized is some concrete national ideal, and is therefore not artificial. Family (*Geschlecht*) is the source of authorization in the Race-State: "the ruler rules because he is the spiritual and material heir of the family which acquired this power through natural superiority;" the maintenance of hereditary rights is the chief political end of this State. In the Form-State the birth of the sovereign is the sole source of his power and right; this State is characterized by the dominance of formal over actual relations.

[1] *Op. cit.*, secs. 209–210.   [2] *Ibid.*, secs. 216–230.   *Ibid.*, p. 352.

The succession of these types of State-constitution in history brings us back again to the age relation existing between the four political types,[1] though the main course of political evolution is still, according to Rohmer, within the second age.   In earliest history we find Idol-States: the priest-states of India and Egypt, the Persian despotism, the Jewish theocracy.   Since then the general line of development has been towards the Individual-State, though particular States have passed prematurely through the two succeeding stages and so have disappeared from the scene of action.   "Personal freedom and the struggle for personal freedom, the living ideas of individuals and the living ideas of nations, become the content of history."[2]   Through Greece and Rome mankind became politically free; with Christianity came religious freedom. "On the firm basis of Christianity, which secured to him the right relations to God, man was able . . . to strive towards an ever higher knowledge of the world and himself, to an ever wider assertion of the dignity of humanity, to an ever completer realization of individuality in the State.   In this endeavor mankind is still employed."[3]

4. VOLGRAFF

K. Volgraff, in his comprehensive ethnological and political philosophy,[4] has, like Welcker and Rohmer, a four-fold scheme for the interpretation of the distinguishing features of the various races and State-systems, based on a primary four-fold anthropological classification. But unlike them he does not correlate his four types

---

[1] *Op. cit.*, secs. 224–30.   [2] *Ibid.*, p. 368.   [3] *Ibid.*, p. 369.

[4] *Erster Versuch einer Begründung sowohl der allgemeinen Ethnologie durch die Anthropologie wie auch der Staats- und Rechts-Philosophie durch die Ethnologie oder Nationalität der Völker.* 3 vols. 1851–05.   References are to the second edition, 1864.

with the corresponding ages of the individual man, though he does, in a general way, treat these types as representing different stages of development and as thus normally succeeding each other in a fixed order.   His system is based on his anthropological doctrine of the four cardinal human temperaments.   These temperaments arise from the difference in fulness and vigor of manifestation of the instinct of self-preservation in the broadest sense of the word.   From the study of anthropology he discovers that all the activities and efforts of man are rooted in the " natural instinct of self-preservation " (*natursittlichen Selbsterhaltungstrieb*), and that this motive of self-preservation has four directions : (1) towards physical well-being in this life, (2) towards psychic-moral well-being in this life, (3) towards perpetuation, after death, but in this world—that is, through reproduction, (4) towards psychical perpetuation, after death, and not in this world.[1]   All the phenomena of human life—all industry, culture, politics, art, philosophy, religion—are simply expressions of this natural instinct of self-preservation.   But this instinct in all phases of its directions expresses itself with different strength and energy in different men ; and from these gradations of the " life-energy " of this instinct are derived the four "primary temperaments " (*Ur-temperamenten*) of the human species.   These four chief types are ethnological as well as anthropological, and are distinguished according to the ascending degree of energy and vigor of the instinct, of its susceptibility to outer stimulation, of the number and variety of the needs and desires that it creates, of the persistence and permanence of its manifestations.   They are designated as the slug-

[1] *Op. cit.*, vol. i, sec. 34.

gish (*träge*), the vivacious (*regsame*), the more practically active (*thätig*), and the ardent or fervid (*lebhafte* or *feurige*).[1] According to this basis of classification humanity as a whole is found to be distributed into four chief races, each race into four classes, each class into four orders, each order into four tribes (*Zünfte*): the "temperamental" differences in each division are indicated in distinctions of religion, culture, civilization, and political organization.[2] The second volume of the treatise is devoted to a detailed working-out of the scheme and an exhaustive application of it to the existing races of men.

B. *THE STATE AS PERSON*

5. STAHL

The political theory which attributes to the State the essential elements of human personality appears in various forms and is deduced from different premises. Friedrich J. Stahl, in his *Theory of Law and the State* (1830–3),[3] bases his interpretation of the State-personality, as also his general theory, on the conception of the "moral realm" (*sittliche Reich*).[4] This moral realm, he tells us, means a " conscious rule, self-unified dominion, according to morally-intellectual motives, over freely-obeying beings who are by the fact of this dominion spiritually unified; a rule which, therefore, spiritually unites these beings; it is accordingly, dominion of personal character in every respect, a realm of personality."[5]

---

[1] *Op. cit.*, secs. 42–49.   [2] *Ibid.*, vol. ii, secs. 1–3.

[3] *Rechts- und Staatslehre auf der Grundlage christlicher Weltanschauung*, 2 vols.   References here are to the third edition, 1854–6.

[4] Vol. ii, p. 1.

[5] " Dieser ist bewusste, in sich einige Herrschaft nach sittlich intellektuellen Motiven über bewusste, frei gehorchende Wesen, damit auch

This moral realm governs man in the religious, ethical, and legal spheres of his life. In its perfect realization it is the kingdom of God; here its personality is manifested in God; the freely obeying beings are Christians who, through the power of God, are made one in spirit with him and with each other. With reference chiefly to the inner life of men while in this world, the moral realm manifests itself in the ethical commands of God, the natural, temporal punishments for sins, and the common ethical ends of men. Finally, the civil order is also a moral realm.

Here also is a dominion established over men and with a personal character—that is, with consciousness of itself and with power of action; it becomes here the rule of an actual, natural personality supported by an organized institution— the State-organism; for the perfect, or, at least, normally natural character of this dominion is that it should have its innermost centre in a natural personality—the royalty. Here also there is a rule of morally rational ends, and here also should men freely obey, since the morally rational order which stands above them is at the same time their own true nature and will and realizes itself only through and in them; and men should through submission to this order and its spirit be united with each other.[1]

In this conception of the moral realm in its political form are thus comprised the three essential elements of the State: a real personal authority over men, with claims to their obedience and allegiance; the morally rational content of that authority, limiting it and standing above

diese geistig einigend—er ist demnach Herrschaft von persönlichen Charakter nach jeder Beziehung, ein Reich der Persönlichkeit." Vol. ii, p. 1.

[1] *Ibid.*, pp. 2–3.

prince and people—that is, the law of the State, the constitution; and, finally, the nation—the people freely obeying the law as an expression and demand of their moral nature and created through their custom and tradition.

The State thus is a "political person" with capacity to act and to rule, as distinguished from a juristic person characterized only by being the possessor of legal capacity and property rights (*Vermögensubjekt*).[1] The State is not, however, an organism. The parts of an organism are definite and distinct in number, location, and function, mutually supplementing and dependent upon one another. They have no independent existence, and the organism exists as such only by virtue of the existence of the parts. "The moral realm, and therefore the State, on the other hand, contains an unlimited number of similar independent existences which neither presuppose one another nor are indispensable to the conception of the realm itself."[2] In the same sense we speak of "natural kingdoms"—the plant kingdom, for example. None of the various species of plants are essential to the existence of the other species, or to the fact or conception of the plant kingdom as such; yet all plants are a part of that kingdom and are subject to its laws. 'A realm, or kingdom, thus, is the sum of similar forms into the life of all of which a higher ruling spirit is incorporated, which, therefore, rules them; "for all rule is the taking up of the thinking and willing of the ruler into the being of the ruled."[3]

The organic feature of the State appears only in the government (*Herrschaft*) of the State. "The government of the State . . . is a moral organism. . . . Princes,

---

[1] *Op. cit.*, p. 18.   [2] *Ibid.*, p. 9.   [3] *Ibid.*

estates, courts, magistracies supplement one another; the
State-government is not complete if the one or the other
of these is lacking, and where these are all present, it is
itself perfect." [1]   As in every organism, the superior and
controlling position must be held by one definite organ;
this is the ruler—the prince, the person actually at the
head of the government. [2] "The government of the
State, consequently the State itself, becomes personal in
the king." [3]   "In the prince the State is personal, without the prince it is no person." Not only the State in
general, but the particular constitution and the particular person of the sovereignty have the sanction of God. [4]

6. SCHMITTHENNER

Closely related to Stahl's idea of the moral realm—of
a spiritually uniting rule directed towards morally rational
ends—in its political form of State-personality, is Schmitthenner's conception of the personal character of the
State, a conception which he regards as a necessary
supplement to the description of the State as an ethical
organism. The customary distinction, Schmitthenner
says, between person and thing is two-fold: in the
first place, person is a being endowed with a moral
destiny for itself as distinguished from that which
has only a destiny for something else; and, secondly, it
is endowed with freedom of the will. But, according to
Schmitthenner, only the former distinction is correct
and essential. For, in the first place, an undeveloped
child is, as having a moral destiny for itself, a person;
yet it is without freedom of the will. Secondly, we can
conceive of beings which might have the fullest capacity

[1] *Op. cit.*, pp. 9-10. [2] *Ibid.*, p. 536.
[3] *Ibid.*, p. 236. [4] *Ibid.*, p. 177.

of free action and yet lack moral destinies for themselves; such beings we call "elfs, goblins, . . . evil spirits," never persons. "We call *person*, therefore, that which has a moral destiny for itself; in other words, that which embodies an objective moral idea." Further, the physical person is to be distinguished from the "merely moral person." The former has physical life and the faculty of action itself, through the free exercise of its own will. The latter has no physical existence as such, no capacity of action itself; it is operative only through organs; and these organs are not determined in their action through the will of the moral person, but through the consciousness of their organic duties—duties, that is, which are established for them through the idea of community (*Gemeinheit*).[1]

7. STEIN

Several decades later, Lorenz von Stein, an author in the field of philosophical public law, bases his theoretical system of State administration, as set forth in his *Theory of Administration* (1864),[2] and *Handbook of Administration Theory* (1870),[3] on the idea of State-personality. In his interpretation of personality the notions of self-ground and self-end form, as with Schmitthenner, an essential part. But the elements of central consciousness and will are also fundamental. The conception, with Stein, implies, in addition to peculiar destiny, life consciously self-determined. The State as person is distinguished from the individual human person through its higher degree of conscious self-determination.

[1] *Grundlinien des allgemeinen staatsrechts*, pp. 260-2.

[2] *Die Verwaltungslehre*, 8 Bde. References here are to the second edition (1869) of the first volume.

[3] *Handbuch der Verwaltungslehre und des Verwaltungsrechts*, 3 Bde. References here are to the third edition (1887).

Stein's construction of the personality of the State is critically and philosophically derived, and throughout his further exposition the implications of the original definition are systematically employed in the analysis of the institutions of the State and of the organs and functions of administration. To define the State, he says, we seek, as a starting-point, what is clearly common to all States, whatever their degree of development; we find this to be the community of men (*die Gemeinschaft der Menschen*). This element is original; it is not something formed by, or introduced among men; "it is given with the existence of mankind."[1] For a peculiarity of the life of man is that he can not completely attain his destiny through his individual powers alone. An absolute condition to such an achievement is an association with other similar individuals, a union of his faculties with theirs.[2] If this alliance of men is to supply what the individual lacks for the accomplishment of his destiny, it must partake of the nature of individual man—it must become a personality. If, furthermore, where there is mankind there also is the community of mankind, if the conception of the former is unthinkable except in connection with the latter, the latter must be "an emanation from the same essence" as the former; the same thought or act of divinity must have created both the individual and the community. The community must therefore have a nature like that of the individuals of which it is composed.[3]

The community of men "raised to personal consciousness and will," to "self-determined personality," is the State.[4] Other theories of the State, Stein maintains,

[1] *Die Verwaltungslehre*, p. 3.
[2] *Ibid.*, pp. 10-11.
[3] *Ibid.*, pp. 3-4.
[4] *Ibid.*, p. 4.

have the common fallacy of overlooking this self-determining personality of the State, and of thus attempting to derive their conception of the State from some other more fundamental conception. They have thus sought to explain the State as a product of human sociability, or as an institution of law for the protection of the rights of individuals, as an expedient in the interests of human welfare, or as a postulate of the moral law. But

the State is not an institution (*Anstalt*), or a requirement of law (*Rechtsforderung*), or an ethical form (*Gestaltung*), or a logical concept,—any more than the ego of mankind. It is a form of personality—the highest material form. It is its essence to have its ground in itself. It can as little be demonstrated (*bewiesen*) or grounded (*begründet*) as the ego. It is itself. One can develop neither it nor the ego from something else; . . . . . . the community of mankind, outside of and above the will of the individual, has its own independent and self-active existence. The State has, therefore, by no means, as the former philosophy says, merely a destiny; . . . it has also a life. Its life lies in its free self-determination.[1]

The personality of the State differs from individual personality not in content, but in degree of self-determination; it is thus a higher form of personality. Elements of personality which in the individual exist only in kernel and undeveloped, appear in the State as " independent organisms endowed with their own form, content, and independent destiny for the whole."[2] But the State—as personality, self-determining, and as ego, conscious of being its own ground—yet exists in a world of outer being which acts upon the State. To maintain its personality—its self-determining nature—the State must " so shape the controlling forces of the outerworld,

[1] *Op. cit.*, p. 5.   [2] *Ibid.*, p. 8.

which it can not set aside, as to make this influence a determining of the ego through itself."[1] This it does through its will. The State realizes its will through action (*That*). "As soon as the self-determination becomes action and thereby subjects the outer-world to itself, we call it life."[2]

In Stein's more concrete analysis of this conception of the personality of the State, we discover its application to the actual constitution of the State in its three powers, or organs. The ego, which in the individual is without independent or distinct existence, appears in the State as the sovereign (*Staats-oberhaupt*), "which in the kingship attains its perfect (*vollendete*) form."[3] The will, in the individual finding expression only in association with other manifestations of life and incapable of revealing itself independently of its expression, has in the State its distinct and peculiar organ, the legislative body, which, through the independent actions of deliberation and resolution, produces law (*Gesetz*)—"the externally existing fact of the will of the State."[4] The next step is the extension of the will, made objective in the law, into the external world. The instrument for this process is the "administrative organism" (*Verwaltungs-organismus*).[5] By this term Stein means both the organ of the "executive" function and that of "administrative" function, in the narrower sense of the word. This "great organism of the activity (*That*) of the State" has two elements, one bearing relation primarily to the State itself in its activity, and one related rather to the outer objects to which this activity is directed. For, in the first place,

---

[1] *Op. cit.*, p. 9.   [2] *Ibid.* Cf. *Handbuch*, pp. 11–12.
[3] *Die Verwaltungslehre*, p. 9.   [4] *Ibid.*
[5] Cf. *Handbuch*, pp. 5, 22.

there must be the will and the force to carry out the will of the State, as expressed in the law, against all resistance. The organ of this will and force is the "executive power;" its will is the "ordinance" (*Verordnung*); its action, the "execution" (*Vollziehung*). "The ordinance is, therefore . . . the willing of the will (*das Wollen des Willens*) of legislation; execution is the doing (*Thun*) of this will through the executive power."[1] But, in the second place, the external world is not merely the object of the will and action of the State; it has its own life, laws, and forces; these must be adapted to the ends of the State, must be dominated by, and made serviceable to, the State.

This process, through which the execution gives to outer things the State's personal ends, as set forth in the laws, is called the administration (*Verwaltung*). The administration is, therefore, the organic activity of the State in the world of real things; its essence—its concept—is that in it the will of the State, the law, through the force and action of the State, the execution, attains realization in the objective fundamental relations of the actual State-life.[2]

The ultimate aim of the administration is always one, namely, the subjection of the whole domain of the life-relations of the State to the personality of the State; its special tasks vary according to differences in the character of these relations.

As indicated above, the "higher" character of the personality of the State consists partly in the fact that the several organs of the State have each a more distinct and independent field of functions than have the organs of the individual human person. Each organ of the State

---

[1] *Die Verwaltungslehre*, p. 10.   [2] *Ibid.*

has an existence complete in itself, and "according to its nature, through its special activities, contains and realizes the life of the State."[1] But it is always the life of the whole whose functions the special organ is to perform. It is a sign of perverted action and of an unhealthy condition, an indication of future dissolution, when any organ directs its activity towards its own ends, or withdraws itself from participation in the general State activity. "No organ can will or act for itself alone; each organ, even the State-sovereign, must at every point of its will and action be and will the whole."[2] There can be, thus, a "separation of powers" only if by "power" is meant "the function of a particular State-organ for and in the name of the whole."[3]

This conception of the self-dependence, not independence (*Selbständigkeit*, not *Unabhängigkeit*), of each special organ determines the content of public law (*Staatsrecht*). Law (*Recht*) is the "inviolability of one personal life through the action of another;"[4] this inviolability is the condition of development. But as the inviolability of one personal life by another, and as the condition of personal life and development, law is "a consequence of the active life of personality,"[5] and its content depends upon the nature and life-relations of the personality of which it is the law. Public law can, therefore, be discovered only from a knowledge of the nature of the State. Furthermore, as the State-personality is characterized by the independent life of its several organs, these organs have their reciprocal limits of activity, each their special law.

It is accordingly clear that the State-sovereign, the legislature,

[1] *Op. cit.*, p. 13.   [2] *Ibid.*   [3] *Ibid.*, p. 16.
[4] *Ibid.*, p. 21.   [5] *Ibid.*

and the administration have each their peculiar (*besonderes*) law, which determines the limits—corresponding to their organic nature—of their peculiar will, their peculiar action, their peculiar life . . . Public law is the arrangement, conceived (*aufgefasste*) and determined as law, of the organs and their political (*staatlichen*) activities in so far as they constitute the unity of the State; it is the limit of the end and activity of each individual organ established through its unity, in conception and operation, with all the others.[1]

Here again the law of any organ becomes known only from a knowledge of "the living and organic nature of that organ,"[2] and of its relations to the other organs. "Each organ finds its limit where this limitation becomes a condition of the function of another organ."[3] The public law becomes positive public law when the State becomes conscious of the nature and relations of the organs and of the limits of their activity, and gives to it all formulations—which make up the *constitutional laws* of the State. This consciousness first arises out of some conflict among the three primary organs of the State, one seeking to dominate another or to extend its activity into the domain of another. The character of the constitution is determined by the interrelation of these three organs and their functions. With the appearance of the constitution, then, the State becomes consciously self-determining in its activity and development. "The constitution raises the State above the natural process of development into the sphere of free spiritual self-determination; it is the highest act of the State; it is the act through which the personality gives itself, with full consciousness, its own nature (*Wesen*)."[4]

[1] *Op. cit.*, p. 23.   [2] *Ibid.*, p. 24.
[3] *Ibid.*, p. 23.   [4] *Ibid.*, p. 25.

8. LASSON

Adolph Lasson, in his *Principle and Future of International Law* (1871),[1] insists upon the realness of the personality of the State and the freedom of the conception from any fictitious or metaphorical sense. "The State," he says, "is person in full earnest; it is person just like any adult living man in his sound senses,"[2] the differences between the State and man not making either any less of a person. However, Lasson does distinguish "moral" from "physical" personality in several respects, and reaches conclusions in the domain of public law and ethics, on the basis of the distinction.

He places the State in the most elevated position among social personalities in general, which he calls "moral persons." This term denotes all such forms of associate life as have an end (*Zweck*) which is primarily distinct from the particular ends of the associated individuals, and which is yet of such intimate concern to the latter as to impel them consciously to offer their intellectual and physical faculties for its attainment.[3] For such an end has the three essential attributes of personality as defined by the jurists with reference to man as a subject of rights; a *Subjekt von Rechten* must have

(1) a will which may set its own end to itself, (2) intelligence for selecting the means corresponding to this end, and (3) the physical capacity (*Vermögen*) to bring about, by means of its will guided by intelligence, definite and tangible consequences in the outer world of facts, and to experience influences from the outer world . . . . When living men, as mandatories and servants of a will which is apart from them and which they recognize as such follow an end which is not their own; when

[1] *Princip und Zukunft des Völkerrechts*, pp. 122–140.
[2] *Ibid.*, p. 124.　　　　[3] *Ibid.*, pp. 127, 129–130.

they, for its realization, choose, through their intelligence, the
means adapted to this end, and place at its demands their own
physical powers . . . , this end acquires those attributes which
make a man a person ; namely, will, intelligence, and power—
which, because they are placed at *its* command, become *its*
will, *its* intelligence, and *its* power.[1]

Only such ends attain this personality as naturally find
their organs in the will, intelligence and physical power
of men; moral persons can not, therefore, be artificially
created by man; they are "given in nature."[2]

The moral person is thus not endowed with its own
peculiar faculties; and though it "exists really, in the
same sense as a physical person,"[3] yet it is a "particular
sort of person"[4] and is to be distinguished from the
physical person in several respects. In the first place,
though like the physical person it is a "willing being,"
it has not a perceptive faculty, feeling, reason, or consciousness. It is, furthermore, not free to choose its
end: its end is definite and determined for all times;
without its particular end it would not exist, for that
end constitutes its nature and its individuality. It follows from this that the moral person can never act in
the interests of the physical persons of which it is composed, "for only as an end distinct from the ends of the
latter, through whose efforts it is realized, has it its
reality."[5] Secondly, because of the non-freedom of its
will and the fixity and singleness of its end, the conduct

---

[1] *Op. cit.*, pp. 126–28.

[2] *Ibid.*, p. 125. *Cf.* p. 129: "Jeder Zweck, der nicht ursprünglich
der Zweck bestimmter einzelner Personen ist, so dass sie für denselben
als für ihr eigenes Interesse handeln, sondern der die Personen zu
seinem Dienern macht—jeder solcher Zweck ist eine moralische
Person."

[3] *Ibid.*, p. 129.   [4] *Ibid.*, p. 132.   [5] *Ibid.*

of the moral person can not be ethically judged. It knows only its own end, and nothing of higher and lower ends; it can act only self-interestedly (*eigennützig*). Its end is one of general well-being, but in acting towards this end it acts exclusively for itself and ignores other ends of general well-being.[1] Thirdly, the moral person can do no legal wrong. The command of a moral person which has a legal form (*Rechtsordnung*) agrees naturally with the conditions of this legal organization and "demands, therefore, that all means chosen for the realization of its end should be conformable to its law. Such means are also alone expedient, for the moral person which puts itself in contradiction with its legal order cannot exist. Only a legal (*rechtliches*) act is therefore an act of the person; what happens illegally can never be ascribed to it."[2] Finally, the most essential distinction between the moral and the physical person lies in the fact that the former can act only through physical persons; it attains actuality only through the intelligence and force of these, its representatives. When the latter act in this capacity, and "in full understanding of their commission and within the limits of their competency," their act is regarded as that of the moral person which they represent, and they themselves are not responsible.[3]

The State is distinguished from all other moral persons by its character of sovereignty above all other persons, moral and physical. The State is "the ultimate source of all law (*Recht*) for all other physical and moral persons; for without its will and its confirmation no law whatever has validity, as it in last instance centralizes within itself all power for realizing law." All other

[1] *Op. cit.*, p. 133.   [2] *Ibid.*   [3] *Ibid.*, p. 134.

attributes of the State follow logically from its character as sovereign moral person.[1]

The State is not the nation (*Volk*) nor is the will of the State identical with the will of the whole people or of the majority. The State-will finds its manifestation in the will of "the sovereign"—he, or they, who for the time being constitutionally represent the State. The sovereign's will is the State-will in so far as the sovereign holds itself within the competence assigned to the sovereign by the "statute" formulating the end of the State and the means of its realization.[2] All power (*Gewalt*) is concentrated in the representative of the State; all political functions are assigned by the sovereign; to the sovereign pertains ultimately and originally all judicial, legislative, and executive authority.[3]

9. GIERKE.

Otto Gierke, in his *German Association Law* (1873),[4] is chiefly concerned with the juristic significance of the personality of the State.[5] However, like Lasson, he shows that according to the German conception the personality of a community or association, and of the State in particular, is entirely real, not fictitious or hypothetical, as Roman legal doctrine represented it to be. The State, or other collective person, is a living union of parts—the general, or social, parts—of the personalities of the individual members. In every form of association —religious, cultural, political, racial—there is a real and independent "community" life, consciousness, and will, over against and distinct from, the lives, conscious-

---

[1] *Op. cit.*, p. 136.   [2] *Ibid.*, pp. 136–37.   [3] *Ibid.*, pp. 139–140.
[4] *Das deutsche Genossenschaftsrecht*, 3 vols.
[5] *Cf.* especially vol. ii, pp. 24–42, 831–874.

nesses, and wills of the individual members of the group.
The State is, as will appear below, distinguished from
other associations by its "higher" position—higher in
respect to power and sovereignty.

In his essay on *The Fundamental Ideas of Public Law
and the Latest Theories of Public Law* (1874),[1] Gierke's
explanation of the personality of the State (personality
being defined as "unity of essence"—*Einheitlichkeit des
Wesens*)[2] is logically implicated in a more distinctly
organismic theory. Here the State is depicted as of natural origin and development and as a living and integral
complex of organs—each with its special functions naturally determined. Like Stein, Gierke starts with the conception of man as possessing everywhere and at all times
the double character of being both an "individual for
himself" and a member of a generic union (*Gattungs-
verbandes*). The basis of this conception he finds in
historic fact as well as in the inconceivability of the contrary idea. Self-consciousness arises only as man knows
himself as at the same time an individual entity and a
part of a group entity. The content and direction of his
will is determined partly from within himself and partly
by other wills. The aim of his existence comprises both
his own life and that of the community; he is neither
solely end nor solely means. And this community
(*Gemeinschaft*) has complete reality and a unified (*einheitliche*) essence. Every human generic union is a
"natural and actual (*wirkliche*) life-unity," which "combines a number of individuals, through the partial surrender of their individuality, into a new and independent
(*selbständige*) whole. . . . Over the individual-spirit,

---

[1] "Die Grundbegriffe des Staatsrechts und die neuesten Staatsrechtstheorien;" in *Zeitschrift für die gesammte Staatswissenschaft*, vol. xxx.

[2] *Ibid.*, pp. 289–290.

individual-will, individual-consciousness, we perceive in a thousand-fold life-manifestations the real existence of common-spirit, common-will, common-consciousness." [1] This human common-life is not confined to a single kind of association. With the cultural advance of humanity these life-unities increase in number, variety, and complexity; they are subject to growth and decay; they become implicated with each other in their life cycles; smaller unities combine into larger, larger unities absorb —or sub-divide into—smaller.

Among these social existences political (*staatliche*) unions form a class: they may be defined as the associations which execute, through power (*Macht*) and with conscious purpose, the general will. The essential elements of an association of this kind are thus: first, its substance (*Inhalt*)—the general will; secondly, its form of expression (*Erscheinungsform*)—the organized power; thirdly, its purpose (*Aufgabe*)—action with reference to a conscious end (*die zweckbewusste That*).[2] The State is a political form of associate life. It is distinguished from other social bodies—from the minor political associations in particular—by its position above them; for it alone there is no limit through a higher collective existence; all other political unions are subordinate to it; its will is the sovereign general will; it is the highest *Machtverband*.

The State, generically—*i. e.*, political union of some kind, is as old as the individual: "it is inborn in humanity to live politically." The State is "no free creation of the individual but the necessary product of the social forces acting (*sich bethätigenden*) in the individuals." Even when a nation has emerged from the stage in

[1] *Op. cit.*, pp. 301–02.   [2] *Ibid.*, p. 304.

which the State develops entirely as a natural product of the unconscious social instinct, and when the State is changed or even founded by a conscious and designed act of the will, such an act is not the result of a combination of individual wills. It is the act of the general will, and the product is not entirely a new creation; for the individuals constituting the community thus making or changing a State must have been already "politically united in their thought and will." The act is "the unitary act of the general will living in the many individuals and only for a time formless."[1]

The State is thus neither the mere sum of the individuals and smaller unions within it nor a mere product of the acts of these; it has its own real existence; it is "a human social organism with a unified collective life (*einheitlichen Gesammtleben*) distinct from the life of its members." Its life appears only in the life-activity of its elements and its organs—the individuals and the minor associations, which, as parts of the State, have their destiny not in themselves but in the collective-life of the State. This fact neither contradicts the fact of the unity of the State nor is incompatible with the non-political side of the life of individuals and associations. The individual belongs only in part to the State; he has a domain of free existence unassailable by the State. There may be an association which comprises all the individuals of the State, and which is yet entirely independent of the State except in so far as "general power-relations" (*gemeinheitliche Machtverhältnisse*) are concerned.[2] The State is the community absolute and general (*schlechthin Allgemeinheit*) and is sovereign when general interests demanding the exercise of power for their maintenance or furtherance are involved.

[1] *Op. cit.*, pp. 304-5. 　　　[2] *Ibid.*, p. 308.

In the State, as in every organism, "the unity of life manifests itself in this: that simple or complex parts of the whole assume, as organs of the whole, definite functions." In the State, as a highly developed organism, these organs are highly differentiated in structure and action, and work with a large degree of independence in their respective spheres of life; but "in all these organs one central life-individuality is manifested, which as omnipresent and all-determining unity is active in every act of an organ, for which and through which each organ exists and functions, and the existence of which is weakened through temporary conflict of organs, and annihilated when they fall into permanent disharmony."[1] In a natural organism the regular working of the different organs in their varied functions, the unity of life within the whole complex of organs, is accomplished automatically—without conscious control, for the most part. In the State-organism the agency of central and conscious direction is more normal and radical: this is the province of public law (*Staatsrecht*). The determination of the respective fields of competence of the several State-organs, the regulation of the conditions and manner of their activity, the introduction of new organs, the discarding of those which have become superfluous or obstructive—all these ends become under particular circumstances objects of public law; yet in the State-organism also, the structure, composition, and functions, are, at the same time, partly a product of spontaneous and historical processes. The place of each organ in the State is constitutional (*verfassungsmässig*) as well as natural.[2]

---

[1] *Op. cit.*, p. 329.   [2] *Ibid.*, pp. 329-330.

NOTE.—Hugo Preuss, in "Die Persönlichkeit des Staates, organisch

und individualistisch betrachtet," *Archiv für öffentliches Recht*, vol. iv
(1889), pp. 62-100, discusses, with numerous citations of authors, the
various contemporary conceptions of State-personality. He contrasts
especially the organismic and the non-organismic—*i. e.* "individualistic"
or juristic—conceptions.

Contrasted views as to the connections between the organismic and
personality conceptions may be seen in the interpretations of Gerber
and Fricker. *Cf.* C. F. von Gerber, *Grundzüge des deutschen Staatsrechts*, 1865 (references here are to third edition, 1880), *Beilage* I:
"Der Staat als Organismus" (pp. 217-224), and *Beilage* II: "Die
Persönlichkeit des Staats" (pp. 225-334); Fricker, "Die Persönlichkeit
des Staates," *Zeitschr. f. d. ges. Staatsw.*, vol. xxv (1869), pp. 29-50.
Gerber's view is that an adequate understanding of the real personality
of the State does not involve the thesis that the State is an organism.
Though he does not definitively combat the latter theory, he regards it
as superfluous. Fricker, on the other hand, though accepting a qualified interpretation of State-personality, maintains that the only essential
conception of the State is that of its organic character. The difference
between the views of these two authors hinges on their conflicting ideas
as to the relations of State-power to individual freedom and function.
Gerber would exalt governmental organs as the peculiar representatives
of State-personality. He says (*op. cit.*, p. 226): "Der Staat als Persönlichkeit hat eine eigenthümliche Willensmacht, die Staatsgewalt.
Sie ist das Recht zu herrschen, d. h. das Recht, zur Ausführung der
im Staatszwecke liegenden Aufgaben, einen das ganze Volk verbin--
denden Willen zu äussern." Fricker would establish all individual
members of the State as organs equally essential to the State-organism.
He says (*op. cit.*, p. 36): "Dass ein solcher Organismus in sich seine
Einheit hat, aber einmal in die Welt gestellt, sich nicht absolut auf sich
selbtst zurückzuziehen vermag, sondern in Rechtsbeziehungen zu An-
dern treten muss, das macht seine vorläufig angenommene Persönlichkeit aus. Sofern nun diese Einheit und Ganzheit, um derenwillen wir
von Persönlichkeit reden, nicht künstliche geschaffen, sondern natür-
lich gegeben und im menschlichen Wesen begründet ist, haben wir
diese Persönlichkeit nicht als künstliche gedachte, wie es bisher
vorläufig ist, sondern als natürliche Person einer höhern Stufe zu be-
greifen. Dies erhält seine Bestätigung in der Wahrnehmung, dass
diese höhere Person in dem Wechsel der menschlichen Individuen, die
ihre Glieder sind, unverändert bleibt." But (pp. 38-9), "es soll jene
Theorie bekampft werden, die mit Zuhilfnahme der Staatspersönlichkeit
den organischen charakter des·Staats zerstört, indem sie den im Staat
vereinigten Menscheitskreis in zwei einander abstract gegenübergestellte
Stücke zerreist, ein herrschendes Subjekt, den Souverän, und ein be-
herrschtes Objekt, das Volk, sei es dass der Staat in dem Souverän per-

sönificirt, oder dass der Souverän als der Vertreter des persönificirt gedachtes Staates angesehen wird.''

A conciliation of these views appears in Preuss' article, ''Über Organpersönlichkeit,'' *Jahrbuch für Gesetzgebung, Verwaltung und Volkswirtschaft*, vol. xxvi (1902), pt. 2, pp. 103-142. His analysis is not essentially different from that of Gierke.

CHAPTER III

The "Natural Science" of the State

SINCE the middle of the nineteenth century many sociologists have employed the biologist's conception of organism in the explanation of social and political institutions. They have maintained that society is a "natural" organism and have treated its origin and development, its organs and functions, as essentially the same in character as the genesis, organs, and functions of plants and animals. The discussion of the State forms only a subordinate part of the general sociological systems of these authors. An analysis of the ideas of the more influential among them has place here (to be given in the next chapter) because of their application of their organismic theory of society to the State. But antedating these sociologists by several decades, writers more immediately concerned with conceptions of the State had, in their reaction from the dominant artificialism of political theory, made familiar the use of the methods and categories of physical sciences in the analysis of these conceptions and in the interpretation of political relations. Their speculation was not only more thoroughly "naturalistic" in a biological respect than that, already examined, of such theorists as Müller, Leo, and Ahrens, but, moreover, the direct dependence of the State upon the laws of *all* natural phenomena—inorganic as well as organic—was maintained by them. The study of the political aspects of the theories of the social organism should be preceded by a consideration of the representative examples of this earlier political *Naturlehre*. Following this exemplification, from the works of Zacharia, Volgraff, and Frantz, we may appropriately take up the doctrines of the political philosopher who, about the middle of the century, developed the organismic conception in the most comprehensive and exaggerated manner. For though this author—J. K. Bluntschli—borrowed only biological notions from the natural sciences, an exposition of his views is due in connection with the review of the more general *Naturlehre* of the State, because of the affinity his works bear to that school in respect to his distinctly political, not sociological, point of view, and in respect to the more broadly anthropomorphic, rather than merely psychological, sense in which the State is conceived by him as an organism.

1. Zacharia

One of the first to develop in detail the idea of the State as a biological organism was Karl Saloma Zacharia, in his *Forty Books Concerning the State*[1] (1839–42). In this work he has a *Naturlehre* of the State which he declares to be the necessary starting point of political science. Within this *Naturlehre* he includes a "Chemistry," and a "Mechanics," as well as a "Physiology and Biology," of the State. Under the last-mentioned head the notion of the State as an organism is clearly and somewhat completely set forth; and though Zacharia indicates significant differences between the State and the natural organism, he makes extended application of the analogy between the two in his discussions of constitution, government, State offices, and other practical political subjects.

[1] *Vierzig Bücher vom Staate*, 7 vols.

In the section *Concerning Political Natural Philosophy*[1] he says:

States have, just as natural bodies, an outer existence . . . They are subject to the same laws as nature, or the corporeal world in general . . . Political Natural Philosophy is the exposition of the laws according to which States exist in experience. . . . It asks: From what causes are the existence of the State, its properties and its varieties (*Verschiedenheiten*), to be derived? It seeks to demonstrate these causes in the general laws of nature, in the character of the scene of action upon which men live and move, and in the bodily and spiritual endowment of men. It is the introduction to political science.[2]

The section on *Physiology and Biology* is the last of the three sections constituting the sixth book, the subject of which is "The General Laws of Nature in their Relations to the State." Zacharia here explains that the similarity between the State and an organic body of nature is not superficial but is of their very essence. Each is a combination of spirit (*Geist*) and inanimate matter. The foundation for the interpretation of the existence of either must be sought in the end to be realized through that existence. The basic stuff of which each is constituted is organic: a natural organic body is made up of units which nature has fitted for organic development; likewise, the radical elements of the State are organic units—the individual human organisms.[3] Corresponding to the three classes of natural organisms— namely, plants, animals, and men, distinguished respectively, by the preponderance of vegetative, animal, and mental life—we find three classes of States. For as

[1] "Von den politischen Naturlehren," bk. vi, sec. 4.
[2] Vol. i, pp. 182–83.   [3] Vol. ii, p. 10.

in plants the "life-force" (*Lebenskraft*) manifests itself as a mere formative and preserving power, so there are States the integrity of which is secured only through fear—*fear* of a superior *force* which maintains the unity of the State; secondly, states in which the unity rests upon the *interest* of the citizens are to be compared to animals—in which the "life-force" appears as instinct; finally, to man—in whom the "life-force" is *reason*—are to be likened those States "in which everything is directed to the end that each individual citizen may with most freedom unfold and develop his powers and capacities in all directions." [1]   Neither among States nor among natural organisms are these classes sharply distinguished in the transitional forms : political history, as well as natural science, reveals a gradation of forms from the lower to the higher organic types.

Like Müller, Zacharia demands that the State prove and maintain its life by action, movement; and furthermore, like Müller, he seems to think that that manifestation must necessarily be in some form of conflict.   "In every natural organic body the life-force is involved in an incessant struggle with the chemical forces of matter. Inertness, stand-still, is not life, but death, or the harbinger of death.   Likewise, political quiescence is not an indication of a healthy condition of the State-body."   A practical conclusion to be drawn from this is that "within the State there must be always a party of the opposition in order that the government may not forget to keep the interest of the public power in equilibrium with the interests of the individual citizens. . . . There must be a degree of political agitation and restlessness—the means, indicated to man by nature, for making freedom secure." [2]

[1] *Op. cit.*, p. 12.   [2] *Ibid.*, pp. 14-15.

Notwithstanding the resemblances and analogies existing between the State and the natural organic body and
the many respects in which the former shows a fundamental kinship with the latter, still the State-organism
is rather the ideal, than the actual, State. The natural
organic body *is*, the State *should be*, an organism; actual
States represent only varyingly successful human efforts
to realize this ideal. "Organic bodies of nature are in
fact that which they should be in this their peculiar attribute: they are works of the Master. States ought indeed to be organic bodies, but they are in reality only
attempts which have been made, or are being made, by
men to approach, through co-ordinating their reciprocal
legal relations (*Rechtsverhältnisse*), the perfection of an
organic body of nature: they are only works of the
pupils." [1]

This ideal should be the actual goal of all State-craft;
as such it determines the true principles of constructive
politics. In order that the State should be an organism
it must have the primary attributes of vital integrity and
inner efficiency. [2] This means that the relation of parts
to the whole is such that the former stand as mere means
to the latter, and that among the parts themselves there
is an affinity and a general similarity of the sort that exists in the structure of an animal and that enables the
anatomist from a few bones to reconstruct the complete
form of the animal. Thus in the State "a single idea
should animate the whole; the same forms should repeat
themselves in different parts of the constitution; the
principles according to which the rights of the majority
are exercised should be of the same general spirit and
character." [3] But a further essential organic quality

[1] *Op. cit.*, p. 11.   [2] *Ibid.*   [3] *Ibid.*, p. 15.

which must pertain to the State, if it is to be an organism, is that of mechanical perfection. In the natural organism, in connection with its primary organic characteristic of inner efficiency, of a general appropriateness of means to end, there is also perfection of mechanism—a completely articulated system for the operation and control of the means. This mechanical perfection in the State is obtainable only through a definite constitutional arrangement. This is to be sought both in the form of government and in the form of sovereignty. The form of government is mechanically complete only under the following conditions: when public offices are relatively few; when the affairs of government are administered by individual officers rather than by collegial magistracies; when the functions of each official are strictly determined and defined by law; when the officials are in close dependence upon the sovereign in tenure and conduct; when the more important public affairs are administered either directly by the sovereign or by his immediate representatives; and when the sovereign can at any time intercept the regular activity of an officer through the power of extraordinary injunction. All this is most completely attainable in the hereditary monarchy—which, therefore, is the proper form of sovereignty.[1] On the other hand, though mechanical perfection of the State-organism is unattainable except through a monarchic and bureaucratic constitution, the State-body should, finally, have the character of a natural organism in the peculiar life enjoyed by each of its parts. As in a natural organic body each part has, though subsidiary to the whole, its own vitality, so each member of the State-body must have its particular life; each branch of the public service,

---

[1] *Op. cit.*, p. 14.

each public magistracy, should within the sphere of action assigned to it by law, enjoy a certain independence. This element of organic perfection may, however, involve peril to the life of the whole; the peculiar life of a particular part may disturb the life, or break up the unity, of the State-body; each magistracy may endeavor to expand its official authority, each branch of the public service may tend to regard itself as the center or crown of the whole. The practical statesman has to steer between this danger and the opposite one of extinguishing the life of an indispensable member of the State. The State-life cannot endure without the persistence of life in its units, the citizens, in the human society comprising these units, and in the public offices performing the manifold tasks in support of the State-life as a whole.

Thus Zacharia regards the complete State-organism— organic completeness being measured according to the standard of higher natural organisms—as an ideal rather than the actuality. Moreover, he recognizes differences as well as analogies between the phenomena of actual State-life and of the life of the natural organism. Nevertheless, he considers life as a fundamental element of the actual State. He conceives the State as capable of organic perfection; but he does not hold that history shows an actual approach towards this end. Yet he has a natural history of the State and under that head presents his ideas of the natural origin and growth of the different kinds of constitution, of the different elements —the "powers"—of the constitution, and of the various legal and economic institutions of the State. The object in this connection is "to present in their sequence the particular events which in their natural course succeed one another in an order determined once for all, and to establish the necessity of this sequence."[1] Absolute predictability as to this process will be always unattainable because of the indeterminate element of free-will inseparable from all life.[2] Political natural philosophy, therefore, "cannot explain all transformations in the State-world. . . . As man, so also his history consists of two elements."[3]

[1] *Op. cit*, p. 237.   [2] *Ibid.*, pp. 234-7.

[3] Vol. 1, p. 186. Krieken (*Organische Staatstheorie*, pp. 75-79) gives a brief abstract of J. C. Planta's *Die Wissenschaft des Staats oder die Lehre vom Lebensorganismus* (1852). Planta attempted to base his political philosophy upon a principle adequate to explain the relations of all phenomena. This fundamental and universal principle is that of polarity (*Polarität*). All objects, animate or inanimate, physical or psychical, are by nature essentially incomplete and in need of mutual supplementation. There is, consequently, a constant *striving-for-each-other* (*Zusammenstreben*) among objects. Every thing, or group of things, stands in a relation of polarity to other things, or groups of things. There is in every object a "being-for-itself" (*Fürsichsein*)—which is its "negative," or "feminine," pole, and a "being-for-another" (*Fürandersein*)—which is its "positive," or "masculine," pole. In inanimate nature the principle of polarity is manifested chiefly in the operations of electricity and magnetism. The polar force of organic nature is distinguished by its character of inner activity and by its greater freedom; in other words, in organic nature it is a *living* force. The State is an organism in that, first, the movements of its polar action of combination, co-operation and supplementation are of a living sort—that is, free and impelled from within; secondly, in that it has a soul, and is endowed with organs related to its needs and with the capacity of conscious self-determination. The polar activity within the State is further conditioned by the co-existence of two opposing political tendencies: one, the masculine, is the principle of "individuality or subjectivity" (*das Individualitäts- oder Subjectivitäts-Prinzip*)—which is the liberal, or rational tendency; the other, the feminine, is the "principle of totality or objectivity" (*das Totalitäts- oder Objectivitäts-Prinzip*)—which is the conservative, or emotional (*Gefühls*) tendency. As in all other natural objects, the degree of harmony between the two poles determines the stage of development of the State. These opposite principles are embodied in political parties. The decline of the State sets in when either of these principles is perverted into its extreme;

2. VOLGRAFF

We have already briefly considered K. Volgraff's four-fold anthropological scheme for the interpretation of the State and its elements, and the classification of its forms.[1] He does not, however, confine himself to that general, primarily psychological, exposition, but combines with it, in his same discursive treatise, conceptions and methods of the natural sciences, and attempts to explain the constitutional organization of the State by analogies (analogies crudely contrived and inconsistently worked out) drawn from the domain of "natural" organisms. The political philosopher, he says, must have a thorough knowledge of all the natural sciences, and should study and explain his particular field according to the methods followed in them; all theories should be verified by observation, especially in the peculiar form that observation must chiefly take here, namely, that of historical investigation.[2]

That all men are endowed with the same natural instincts and motives, but with different degrees and kinds of ability, is the ultimate explanation of social and political life. Men live together because they are dependent

that is, when conservatism and emotionalism degenerate into absolutism, or liberalism and rationalism degenerate into radicalism.

The soul of the State is the collective political consciousness of the nation; legislation is the heart, and government the brain; through legislation and government the reasons and wills of the people are combined into organs adapted to the needs of the State. A harmoniously developed State is distinguished from other states as man from beasts; that is, through its self-consciousness and its capacity for self-determination. This determination is expressed in its constitution, which defines its character—its fundamental arrangement (*Anlage*), and regulates the relation between the State-soul—the national political consciousness—and the State power, as incorporated in the system of State-organs.

[1] *Supra*, p. 60.   [2] *Op. cit.*, vol. i, sec. 3.

upon one another in the satisfaction of their needs. Human societies are formed as instinctively and spontaneously as are animal and plant societies, the only essential distinction being that in the higher stages of the former the members are conscious of some of the formations that are taking place.[1]   Where voluntary contracts and laws appear they are not creative agencies, but merely regulative measures and expressions of earlier and involuntary changes in political relations.[2]   A civil society, forming itself thus naturally from the mutual needs of its members, cannot endure without "protecting organisms," which prevent dissolution within and destruction from without.[3]   The "natural political organism" is the "organic constitution," the "State-form."[4] In the plant and animal kingdoms organism signifies that interpenetration (*Ineinandergreifen*) and co-operation of the various individual organs, upon which the total existence, the life-process and permanence, of the whole is dependent.   In political societies the analogue of this organism is the constitution or "State-form."[5] Notwithstanding that this political organism is a means to the end of civil society, it is no more arbitrary or optional than the plant or animal organism—which exists as the means to the end of the plant or animal life.   It is given in the nature of political society.   In its origin and development it bears a natural and essential correlation with the cultural stage of the society whose organic form it constitutes.   So-called organic constitutional laws only confirm what a cultural-political demand has already produced.[6]

This political organism, the organic constitution or

---

[1] *Op. cit.*, vol. ii, sec. 1.   [2] *Ibid.*, secs. 2–3.   [3] *Ibid.*, sec. 23.
[4] *Ibid.*, sec. 32.   [5] *Ibid.*, p. 106.   [6] *Ibid.*, p. 107.

State-form, is itself composed of four " organisms "—the four permanent and indispensable organisms of every political society.[1] These are (1) the civil (*Staats-bürger-liche*) organism, (2) the organism of the administration of justice, (3) the organism of taxation and finance, and (4) the military organism. By the first[2] is meant the classification of the members of the State according to the distinctions in their capacity for service in the maintenance of the political society; these distinctions being based on the natural differences in age, sex, physical and mental faculties, and on the resulting differences in acquired efficiency. Through this organization to each is assigned the political functions for which he is qualified, as in Plato's system of political justice. It is for the State what the physiological system (*Physiologie*) is for the physical body, " in so far as to each part its appropriate place and appropriate functions are adjusted."[3] No human volition or designed act is needed in this political classification: " It is the essence of things, nature, which here separates, classifies, grades, and organizes."[4] By the organism of the administration of justice[5] is meant the organization of the members of society whereby is obtained the punishment of malefactors against the State and the settlement of controversies in matters of marriage and family, labor, property, inheritance and exchange. It is like the sanative force (*Heilkraft*) of the physical body, " for through it all

---

[1] *Op. cit.*, p. 136. The author calls them " organisms "; if he had cared to employ the analogy in greater detail or more precisely he would probably have designated them as the four systems of organs.

[2] *Ibid.*, secs. 34–36.

[3] *Ibid.*, p. 112, note *e*. In this note are also indicated the biological analogies of the other three " political organisms."

[4] *Ibid.*, p. 119.   [5] *Ibid.*, sec. 37.

inner derangements of society—as when individuals by their conduct isolate themselves, as it were, from the whole—are restored to normal conditions." The organism of taxation and finance [1]—the system by which disbursements from the various public funds are made and recuperated from taxation or public property, is to be compared to the system of nutrition in the physical body. Finally, the military organism [2] is the organization of the defense of political society. It is to be likened to " the instinct of self-preservation of all bodily organs, since they all function and tend towards warding off the injurious from without and discarding foreign materials from the body." Though these essential organisms are present—in embryonic, if not fully developed form—in all political societies, the completeness and perfection of organization in any given society corresponds to the stage of its cultural development. [3]

These organisms are not mere dead forms or systems; they are living and active. The " living functions " of the four organisms constitute together the public power (*öffentliche Gewalt*). [4] This public power has two branches, according as its activity is subjective or objective. The subjective part is the State-power (*Staats-Gewalt*), the objective part the governmental power (*Regierungs-Gewalt*). The former is the morally sovereign (*sittliche herrschende*) element of the State; the latter rules, guides, and directs, but only as servant of the former, and is related to it as the understanding to the heart. [5] The State-power is the whole complex of instincts, emotions, ideas, and cultural and religious ideals of the people. [6] It is " public opinion " in the

---

[1] *Op. cit.*, sec. 38.   [2] *Ibid.*, sec. 39.   [3] *Ibid.*, sec. 41.

[4] *Ibid.*, sec. 93.   [5] *Ibid.*, sec. 94.   [6] *Ibid.*, sec. 95.

broadest sense of the word, and even when not politically
organized in the national assembly, it operates, in sound
political conditions, effectively to restrain or stimulate
the governmental power.[1]   But this State-power, the
heart or soul of the State, is by its nature cumbersome
and unfitted for action or for the detailed direction of
public affairs.   This function of guidance and regulation
is rendered by the governmental power.[2]   It is the reflecting, planning, controlling, and executing part of the
public power, and as such falls to the intellectual,
talented, and accomplished citizens—in other words, to
the natural aristocracy of the nation.   "The governmental power is related to the whole State as the head
to the whole body;" it is therefore an inseparable part
of the State, and derives its functions from no contract;
it is as much a natural element as is the State-power.
"As, however, the head — the seat of all spiritual (*geis-
tigen*) organs of the body—is absolutely dependent upon
the constitution of the whole man, and as spiritual
forces are only the reflex of the psychical life-energy, so
the government is, with regard to what it is within its
competence or duty to do, bound by the will—partly
express, partly implied—of the people."[3]   The government may, therefore, never follow its own caprice or
interest; the well-being of the State forms the norm for
all its actions.

3. FRANTZ.

Constantin Frantz, like Planta, Zacharia, and Volgraff,
endeavors to give to political theory a foundation in a
natural science of the state.   The title of his most important book is *The Natural Philosophy of the State as*

---

[1] *Op. cit.*, p. 218.   [2] *Ibid.*, sec. 103.   [3] *Ibid.*, p. 228.

Basis of all Political Science (1870)[1]; in this he distinguishes the *Naturlehre* from the *Rechtslehre* and the *Sittenlehre* of the State, each of the three forming an essential branch of a *Staatslehre*. The political *Naturlehre* studies the State's physical, natural, elements as distinguished from its legal and moral elements. Furthermore, its methods are those of the physical, natural sciences: it proceeds by observation and analysis of the parts of the State as it is, of the actual State; it views all elements of the State from a natural, physical, standpoint. The State in its origin and development is "natural"; and it has an organic character; but, Frantz points out, if the term "organic" be taken in the ordinary sense of natural science, it can be applied to the State only with a very much qualified meaning; and the organic character is one among other equally fundamental properties of the State. The author therefore indicates wherein those writers err who treat the organic as the sole determining quality of the State, or attempt to make the State's resemblance to plant and animal organisms too sweeping.

Frantz maintains, however, that the principal defect of the prevailing manner of political thinking lies in the disregard, or inadequate and metaphorical treatment, of the "natural side" (*Naturseite*) of the State. The State contains elements which belong to the domain neither of law nor of ethics.[2] "Whatever one may set about in political life, three questions always arise: namely, what can (*kann*) I do? what may (*darf*) I do? what ought (*soll*) I to do?" That is, all State practice, every public undertaking, has to be regarded in its physical, as well

[1] *Die Naturlehre des Staats als Grundlage aller Staatswissenschaft.*
[2] *Ibid.*, p. 6.

as in its legal and moral relations; and "the question of
the 'can' must always come first (*vorausgehen*); its
answer is, therefore, the most important of all."[1] On
this basis we have a division of general political science
into a natural science, a legal science, and a moral science,
and the first is the foundation of the latter two, as truly
as the physical individual is the real substratum of the
legal and moral subject, or as anthropology is the ground
and presupposition of psychology.[2] Rights and duties
in the State have no meaning save in association with
material objects—property, for example—or with the
personality of the citizen—who becomes accessible to
the State only through his quality as a physical individual, for in that capacity alone can the State exercise upon
him the compulsory authority indispensable to all its institutions.

The pure thought and will of man transcend the sphere of the
State, which knows thought and will only as corporealized in
individuals; just as all institutions of the State must in some
way be embodied in men, because pure laws (*Gesetze*) as such
are inefficacious and only form the norm for the mode of
operation of living beings. All legal and moral relations in
the State rest on natural relations, which must, therefore, be
first investigated, if legal science and moral science are not to
degenerate into fallacious abstractions.[3]

The political influences of land, climate, and other physical circumstances come into consideration in this *Naturlehre*, but by no means constitute its principal content. The *Naturlehre* studies the State itself on its
physical side, as the *Rechtslehre* studies it on its legal
side.[4]

[1] *Op. cit.*, p. 7.   [2] *Ibid.*, p. 8.   [3] *Ibid.*, p. 9.   [4] *Ibid.*, p. 13.

"The first principle of a political natural science, . . . its presupposition, with which it stands or falls," is that "the State arises through natural forces, and is, according to its basis, a natural product (*Naturprodukt*)."[1] States have never been founded primarily through the agency of human free will. Elements of physical necessity always appear as the original incentives to State-forming. Cultivation of the soil, protection from wild beasts, defense against hostile neighbors—circumstances such as these are the conditions which make some sort of organized union of men indispensable to their continued existence. The will has place in this unification to the extent that men may, within certain limits, choose the form in which they will unite in obedience to such exigencies. Moral and religious impulses also act as contributory influences, but these, again, do not "issue from the will;" they often oppose themselves to the will with the voice of command. Though the living community (*lebendige Gemeinschaft*) arising from physical, supplemented by spiritual, impulses is the true basis of the State, it is not the State itself. The State, in the full sense of the word, appears only when there is recognition of this common life on the part of the members of the community. This recognition makes the actual (*thatsächliche*) a legal (*rechtliche*), community. When a new state is formed by a people of past political experience and culture, this recognition may be in the form of a contract. "But such a contract does not found the new State community . . . but only gives to it a permanent form, and, so to speak, impresses its seal thereupon."[2]

However, the *natural,* that is the object of the political

---

[1] *Op. cit.*, pp. 14–15.   [2] *Ibid.*, p. 18.

Naturlehre is not the purely material, or "nature" in the ordinary acceptation of the word. This *Naturlehre* has nothing to do with purely physical principles, such as electricity or gravitation. The categories of the ordinary natural sciences cannot be applied to the State life. "The State-life is no image of the telluric or cosmic system, or even of the plant or animal organism." "It is human nature, especially as it appears in the associated life (*Zusammenleben*) of men, . . . those functions and elements which are peculiar to human life,"[1] that the political *Naturlehre* has to deal with. Even within the sphere of human life the field must be further defined, for "the organs and forms of development of the individual man find only a very limited analogy in the State. There can by no means be based upon this analogy such a science of the State as Bluntschli attempted." True, all the parts and forces of the State have in some way their origin in the individual human life, but their formation and manner of operation are quite distinct in the State-life and produce arrangements which have no meaning for individual life. "Where in the individual man can there be found an analogue of the judiciary, the system of taxation, the police, the diplomatic service, and so forth?" On the other hand, there are in the human being members and faculties which have no counterparts in the State: "the State has no sense-organs, no memory, no imagination, and so forth, and it is empty jesting to speak of such."[2] The State is an aggregate life of men (*Gesamtleben der Menschen*), not an aggregate man (*Gesamtmensch*).

[1] *Op. cit.*, pp. 25–26.

[2] *Ibid.*, p. 26. The author continues: "It borders on downright burlesque, for example, when the foreign department is likened, as by Bluntschli, to the nose."

The latter conception would require a surrender on the part of each citizen of his individuality, whereas in the State, properly conceived, this never happens. This does not mean that the State is "the mere sum of relations existing between the citizens;" "it is a body, with a material basis in the State territory (*Staatsgebiet*);" "it forms an entity (*Wesenheit*) for itself." Furthermore, it has an organic character in that, under normal conditions, its growth is maintained through the propagation and multiplication of its elements—the individual men—and its evolution is perpetuated through the transmission of particular customs and dispositions by inheritance from one generation to another.

But Frantz considers that the fact of the organic character of the State is too well established in the political theory of his time to need amplification by him, and it is against the inordinate exaggeration to which that conception has been carried that he directs his argumentation in this connection. A system in which the State is defined as simply an organism, in which the organic quality of the State constitutes its whole nature or forms the most important element therein, obscures the true character of the State and leads to wrong consequences, in theory and in practice. "Accordingly, our proposition is that the State indeed has an organic property which pertains to its essence but is far from forming its entire essence or even its most important property; that it has other equally essential properties which are not merely distinct from the organic property but stand partly in manifest contrast thereto." [1]

What are these non-organic properties of the State? In the first place, the State is architectonic: it contains

[1] *Op. cit.*, p. 28.

an artificial structure (*Kunstwerk, Aufbau*), which is
the organization, through the conscious, premeditated,
work of men, of offices and institutions for the operation of government.[1]   Secondly, the State is mechanical.
The elementary parts of the State, the individual men,
are not, as the elementary parts of the organism, exis-
tent only for the sake of the whole: the State exists for
the individuals, not the individual for the State.   Each
man has a will and life purpose of his own.   To hold
these men together in the State, to overcome the centri-
fugal tendencies of human selfishness, the organic forces
of common descent, tradition, customs, and speech,
are not sufficient; a compulsory power in the State-
authority, to keep them united by force, is indispensable.[2]
The former artificial theories of the State erred simply in
laying exclusive stress upon this mechanical character
and in disregarding the necessary organic elements.
Thirdly, the State has an ethical (*sittlich*) character.   It
has an essential relation to the moral life and must proceed morally in all its acts; there must be a moral ideal
for the State.   Here again the inadequacy of the organismic definition of the State is manifest.   The organic is
physical and therefore subject to the immutable laws of
causality inherent in the physical world.   The ethical is
a spiritual idea and freedom is essential to its conception.
To call the State an "ethical organism" obscures the
spiritual and free nature of the ethical element.[3]   Fourthly,

---

[1] *Op. cit.*, pp. 28–29.   [2] *Ibid.*, p. 30.

[3] *Ibid.*, p. 35.   The Hegelian doctrine of the State as "concrete
morality" is also fallacious, Frantz declares.   Morality is the end of
the State, but is not immanent or realized in the State.   State laws do
not have the authority of moral laws.   "What the State-end demands,
and what takes place in conformity to that demand, is not *ipso facto*
moral."

the State is characterized by continuity of development: this is its historical (*geschichtliche*) property. Besides being subject to the physical *müssen* and the moral *sollen*, the State has this further element of necessity; it cannot rid itself of its connection with its past. It is distinguished here from the organic in that there is no termination, no completion, to its development, whereas the organism is "a being which at some point becomes finished and then remains what it has become".[1]   In the fifth place, history, national type (*Volksart*), and physical environment (*Land*), working together produce a State individuality.   Here again we see a contrast between the State and the organism.   In the former the kind of individual, in the latter the kind of species, is the important thing.   In organisms as such individual differences are of secondary importance; the individual plant or animal reproduces the type of its species with only minor variations.   "For the State, on the contrary, the individual character is as essential as the general, and in practice is everywhere the determining factor".[2] Sixthly, when a State becomes conscious of itself it has attained personality, and this is its final property.   The State, the foundation of which is, as has been shown, necessity, must, if it is to survive and not fall into decay or be absorbed by some other State, be sanctioned by the will.   "Personality, which is individuality become self-conscious, first completes the State".[3]

In actual states these seven properties (the organic and the six non-organic) are variously combined; no enduring State lacks any one of them: in this State one property is pre-eminent, in that State, another.   In patrimonial monarchies, in which almost the whole State-life is concen-

---

[1] *Op. cit.*, pp. 37-38.   [2] *Ibid.*, p. 49.   [3] *Ibid.*, p. 50.

trated in the king, the personal element stands out most prominently. In the larger and more developed monarchies, with their well-defined distinctions of classes and ranks, districts and magistracies, the architectonic property is paramount. Aristocracies are of a more organic character because "the hereditary family-influence pervades the whole public life."[1] In democracies the ethical element comes more into evidence through the agency of public opinion and the free play of intellectual energies. Despotisms, finally, are characterized by the force through which the citizens are held in union and controlled; this gives the despotic State its mechanical character. All states have the necessary historical development.

The organic is thus only one among several fundamental properties of the State; it is not the most essential element in the conception of the State, and only in particular instances is it the dominant characteristic of actual states. "Hardly is there a single relation of human life that is not in some way embraced by the State."[2] Though a complete definition of the State requires the indication of its seven determining attributes, yet, as was pointed out at the beginning, a comprehensive study of the State may be made from any one of three points of view—the physical, legal, or ethical. But while a system of political theory may properly take any one of the three phases of the State as its peculiar field of inquiry, it can never rationally lose sight of the essential connection of that phase with the others, or regard that phase as constituting the whole nature of the State. Each science studies the whole State from its particular standpoint. The *Naturlehre* views all parts

[1] *Op. cit.*, p. 52.   [2] *Ibid.*, p. 53.

of the State from a natural, physical, point of view—
from the standpoint of actuality and force. "Everything
that in any way moves man, from the lowest bodily needs
to the highest spiritual impulses, is considered as a
force."[1]　It studies religious faith as a force, disregarding the object of the faith. It studies the workings of
morality in the State as a force, without invading the
province of political ethics to determine in what the
good or evil of a deed consists. Law, in its origin and
in itself a "form and a norm," becomes, when it has
attained general authority, a force, and as such is in the
field of the *Naturlehre*. It studies the natural workings
of public institutions and statutes, of money, manners,
customs, and traditions, as forces in the State. Finally,
it treats of each political factor according to its natural
origin and development. Its subject-matter is the *actual*,
not the ideal or the just.[2]

4. BLUNTSCHLI

The culmination of the organismic method in political
theory proper may be said to have been reached in the
writings of Johann Kaspar Bluntschli. It is true that in

---

[1] *Op. cit.*, p. 58.

[2] Herman Post, in his various legal treatises, sought to establish a
natural science of law through demonstrating the necessity of employ-
ing the empirical method in the study of political and legal facts, and
through explaining the application of "universal laws" in the interpretation of these facts. In tracing the operation of his fundamental *Welt-
gesetz* in the State he tabulates analogies between features of the State
and phenomena of its organic and inorganic environment. In some
passages he indicates particular similarities between the State and the
organic world. But he nowhere elaborates the comparison or makes
his general political interpretation organismic. *Cf.* his *Ursprung des
Rechts* (1876), especially pp. 1–29 and 136–145. For brief reviews of his
Naturgesetz des Rechts (1867) and his *Einleitung in eine Naturwissenschaft des Rechts* (1872), *cf.* Gumplowicz, *Gesch. d. Staatsth.*, pp. 354–9.

his synthesis of the common and essential characteristics of all States, he, like Frantz, includes other properties than the organic, and he explains in what respects the organic property is not to be understood in its purely, or solely, natural-science sense. But in some of his essays he makes a more exaggerated application of the organismic conception, in the indication of particular analogies between the State and the human organisms, than has been made by any other political philosopher; and in all his theoretical discourse he sustains the organismic doctrine in the most whole-hearted manner. His interpretation of the nature of the State comprehends different organismic points of view singly set forth by other theorists. He insists upon the essentially living character of the State, explains in detail that it has the fundamental attributes of natural organisms, and compares it particularly with the human organism, ascribing to it personality and even sex. The State is the image of man (*das Bild des Menschen*); it is, moreover, the image of a male human being (*das Bild des Mannes*). Finally, his works contain elaborate criticisms of the non-organismic theories of the State.

The organism concept forms a radical element of his *General Theory of the State*,[1] and to the more detailed elucidation and support of this idea he devotes several special essays[2]. In the former work seven properties are specified as the "common characteristics of all

---

[1] *Allgemeine Statslehre.* This forms the first volume of his general work on political theory, public law and politics. His general work appeared first in one volume, 1852; this was later expanded to two, and in the fifth edition, 1875–6, to three, volumes—under the title of *Lehre vom modernen Stat.* An English translation (by D. G. Ritchie, P. Matheson and R. Lodge) of the first volume has been published (second edition, 1892).

[2] *Cf. Gesammelte kleine Schriften.*

States."[1] In every State there is (1) "a multitude of men united", (2) a "State-territory", "a permanent relation of the nation to the soil", (3) a "unity of the whole" so that the State "possesses co-ordinated co-herence in its inner organization and appears as a homo-geneous whole in its relations to other States"; in every State there is (4) a "distinction between governing and governed"; every State has (5) an "organic nature", (6) personality, since it is a "moral-spiritual organism" (*sittlich-geistige Organismus*), and (7) a "masculine char-acter". The form in which Bluntschli's ideas of the human-organic nature of the State are set forth in this and other treatises may best be revealed through a suc-cessive consideration of his reflections, in various parts of his works, on the three last-mentioned properties.

In the first place, the State is a living organism. It "is by no means a lifeless instrument, a dead machine, but is a living, and therefore, organic being . . . This conception refutes both the mathematical-mechanical view of the State, which operates only with numbers, and the atomistic method of treatment, which forgets the whole in the individuals".[2] But the other extreme—the purely biological and naturalistic conception—is to be avoided: the State is not a pure product of nature; it "does not stand on the same grade as the lower organ-isms of plants and beasts, but is of a higher kind".[3] It is "indirectly the work of man," and has a natural basis in the sense that through this work is manifested the natural tendency of man to political life. The realization of this political tendency is accomplished through human agency and human arrangement. "When we call the

[1] *Lehre vom modernen Stat*, vol. i, pp. 14-24.
[2] *Ibid.*, p. 18.   [3] *Ibid.*, p. 22.

State an organism, therefore, we are not thinking of the activity of natural beings in seeking, appropriating, and assimilating nourishment, and in reproducing their kind."[1] Nevertheless, the State is organic in three respects— which constitute fundamental characteristics of natural organisms. These three common organic properties are as follows:

(a) Every organism is a union of corporeal, material elements and vital, psychic forces—in short, of soul and body. (b) Although an organic being is and remains a whole, it is, nevertheless, in its parts endowed with members which are animated by special impulses and capacities, in order to satisfy in various ways the changing life-needs of the whole. (c) The organism has a development from within outwards and an external growth.[2]

The organic union of soul and body is manifested in the State in the embodiment of the national spirit and will in the constitutional arrangement of State-organs.[3] The soul of the State is the spirit of the nation; the constitution is its body. Though a nation is inconceivable except in connection with the aggregate of individual men of which it is composed, yet it is something more than this multitude of men, just as a painting is something more than the sum of the various oils and shades of color of which it is made up, or the tree more than a vast collection of plant cells.[4] The nation, the painting, the tree, each has its distinctive character—an individuality which cannot be explained as the resultant of the common properties of its elementary parts. The individuality of the nation is manifested in the national spirit.[5] Though this aggregate spirit (*Gesamtgeist*) of

[1] *Op. cit.*, p. 19. [2] *Ibid.* [3] *Ibid.*, pp. 19–20.
[4] *Gesammelte kleine Schriften*, vol. i, p. 297. [5] *Ibid.*, pp. 298 *et seq.*

the nation is not to be sought outside of the individual men, in the souls of whom are its elements, yet it is not simply the agreement, or the common thought and feeling, of all the individual souls.   In each man there is a two-fold spirit; each has, besides his individual spiritual life, a part of the spirit of the nation.   These two sides of a man's psychic life often come into conflict with each other, each impelling him in an opposite direction. "Each of us has within himself the opposition of the race and the individual; each has . . . the soul-forces (*Seelenkräfte*) which work in his race—in common with many or all the other men—while his individual spirit exists only singly and has its endowments for itself alone."[1]   Each man lives a two-fold life and has a two-fold destiny towards the fulfilment of which it is his function to work.   In his individual life he manifests and develops his individual character.   On the other hand, the life of each forms part of the common race-life, in participation in which, through the various common activities, each contributes to the manifestation and development of the national character.   "When we perfect ourselves individually we fulfil our individual life-end, and when we work for the perfection of our nation . . . we help to realize the ideals (*Ideen*) which history has set in the development of nations."[2]

The constitution (*Statsverfassung*), with its organs for a representation of the whole which expresses the State-will as law, with a State-head which governs, with many sorts of magistracies and offices for administration, with courts for the exercise of public justice, with institutions (*Pflegeämtern*) of all kinds for the common cultural and economic interests, with the army for expressing the public force—this constitution

[1] *Op. cit.*, pp. 303–4.   [2] *Ibid.*, pp. 304–5.

is the State-body, in the form of which the nation manifests its aggregate life (*Gesamtleben*).[1]

In the articulation of the State-body, or constitution, is revealed the second organic characteristic of the State. The members of this body—the various political offices and assemblies—have each their peculiar function; in executing these functions they normally manifest vitality and spirituality. The parts of the State "are not dead members of a dead system;"[2] the efficiency of an office ceases when its activities are mechanically repeated without respect to the changing needs of the State. "An office is not like a part of a machine; it has not merely mechanical activities, which remain always the same, as have the wheels and spindles of a factory, which always do the same thing in the same way. Its functions have a spiritual character, and they change in particular cases according to the needs of public life, for the satisfaction of which they exist. Serving life, they are themselves living."[3] In each office there is a "spiritual something" (*geistiges Etwas*), a "living breath" (*lebendiges Hauch*).[4] The "character," or "spirit," of the office, as distinct from that of the person who holds the office, is evidenced by the elevating influence which an office has upon the incumbent; irresolute and ordinary men by assuming public office are strengthened and ennobled by the spirit and dignity of the office; for example, "the office of judge is so sacred, so consecrated to justice, that these noble attributes can even animate the soul of a weakling who is appointed to a judgeship, and arouse

[1] *Lehre vom modernen Stat*, vol. i, p. 19.

[2] *Gesammelte Schriften*, vol. i, p. 266.

[3] *Lehre vom modernen Stat*, vol. i, p. 20.

[4] *Gesammelte Schriften*, vol. i, p. 266.

in him the courage to stand up for the right."[1]   This inner organic differentiation of organs and functions forms the true basis of the modern political principle of the separation of powers, and, more than the attainment of security to civil liberty, constitutes the rational justification for the adoption, by the State of to-day, of governmental structures embodying that principle.   The statesman simply follows the example of nature; as the eye is adapted for sight, the mouth for speaking, so the functions of the State-body are better fulfilled when for each function there exists a distinct and appropriately constituted organ.   However, no more in the State than in nature can the separation of organs be complete.   As in the natural body the several members are all bound together, so also in the State the connection of the different organs must be secured.   There must be a unity of State-power.[2]   Furthermore, the various organs are not of equal power.   Subordination of some organs to others is a characteristic of all organisms.   "In all living beings we find a manifoldness of forces and organs, but at the same time a unity in this variety, a superordination of organs, a highest organ in which the unifying direction is concentrated . . . So also in the State one highest organ is a necessary condition of its life, and this cannot be split into parts if the State itself is to remain a unity."[3]   The organ highest in power in the State is the government (*Regierung*), which is related to the other repositories of political authority as the head to the limbs of the human body;[4] "the head cannot be separated from the body or made equal to it without destroying the life of the man."[5]

---

[1] *Lehre vom modernen Stat*, vol. i, p. 20   [2] *Ibid.*, pp. 588–9.
[3] *Ibid.*, pp. 374–5.   [4] *Ibid.*, pp. 594–5.   [5] *Ibid.*, p. 590.

The third respect in which the State is organic is in its growth, along with that of the nation. This concomitant growth of nation and State is a part of the "nationality principle" of the State[1]—the embodiment of a nation in a State. The needs and views of a nation alter with the periods of its life; each age has its peculiar principle and temper. The statesman cannot disregard this fact. The national State accompanies the nation in this development; the State-organism adapts itself to each stage of national evolution without losing its identity; there is no break between the ages—"the collective history of a nation and State is a coherent whole."[2] "The Roman State through all its various changes reveals the character of the Roman people. . . . The English monarchy of the Tudors differed from that of the house of Hanover, because the nation developed between the sixteenth and eighteenth centuries."[3] The similarity of national and State development to that of a natural organism is far from being perfect. The presence of free human agency as a potent factor in political development prevents that regularity of growth and decay which characterizes the life of plants, animals, and men. The variations, accelerations, or retardations, or even reversals, of the normal course of State and national evolution, may be the consequence of the influence of either "great and strong individuals, or the wild passions of the nation itself." "These deviations are neither so numerous nor usually so great that the rule itself thereby becomes meaningless. . . . But they are, nevertheless, important enough to show that the idea of a mere natural growth is one-sided and unsatisfactory, and to make us even in this

---

[1] *Op. cit.*, bk. ii, ch. iv.   [2] *Ibid.*, p. 21.
[3] *Theory of the State*, p. 107.

respect give to the free action of individuals its due weight."[1]   But this distinction of the State from natural organisms does not render it free from the inevitable period of decay and death to which all organisms are subject.[2]   The State is mortal.   The cause of the death of a State is not national immorality, bad government, race mixture, or race degeneracy, or any other circumstantial condition.   "The true cause lies in the great law of all terrestrial organic life—that it is developed and consumed by history.   The life of the nation and of the State unfolds itself, and, in gradually revealing what lies in it, fulfils its destiny and dies, overtaken and left behind by the unwearied advance of time with which it can no longer keep pace."[3]   The particular form of the death of the State may be national dissolution, anarchy, migration, subjugation to another State, voluntary incorporation with another State, voluntary or compulsory division of one State into several States, partition of one State among several other States.[4]

The State is a "higher kind of organism" than plants and animals, not only because of the function of free human agency in modifying its development, but also by virtue of its character as a pre-eminently "moral and spiritual organism . . . a great body which is capable of taking up into itself the feelings and thoughts of the nation, uttering them in law and realizing them in acts." History "ascribes to the State a personality which, endowed with spirit and body, possesses and manifests a will of its own."[5]   It is this fact alone which can explain the devotion of citizens to the State, the willingness of

---

[1] *Lehre vom modernen Stat*, vol. i, p. 22.

[2] *Cf.* bk. iv, ch. v, " Untergang der Staten."

[3] *Ibid.*, p. 320.   [4] *Ibid.*, pp. 320–3.   [5] *Ibid.*, p. 22.

its subjects to sacrifice themselves for the sake of its integrity and its rights. "The joys and sorrows of the State have at all times been participated in by all its citizens. The whole great idea of fatherland and love of fatherland would be unthinkable if to the State there did not pertain this high moral and personal character."[1] The purpose of the constitutional organization of the State is to enable the State-person to formulate and realize its will, which (as has already been shown) is distinct from the sum or average of the individual wills. "The personality of the nation and of the State is independent of the personality of the individual citizens."[2] It is not a "juristic fiction or a poetic metaphor." For the nation, through the State, has in itself both of the essential constituents of the personality of man: "it has a self-conscious spirit and will, which is something other than the sum of the individual wills of all or a majority of the citizens, and it has the capacity for expressing its will in words and deeds through the constitutional organs."[3]

Finally, to the State must be attributed masculinity —as contrasted with the feminine character of the church. "A religious community may have all the other characteristics of a State-community; nevertheless, it does not wish to be, and is not, a State, just because it does not consciously rule itself like a man, and act freely in its outer life, but wishes only to serve God and perform its religious duties."[4] As mankind (*Menscheit*) is never sexless, so "the State cannot be both man (*Mann*) and woman:" for it would not then

[1] *Op. cit.*, p. 23.
[2] *Gesammelte Schriften*, vol. i, p. 91.   [3] *Ibid.*
[4] *Lehre vom modernen Stat*, vol. i, p. 23.

be the image of the human being (*Menschen*); "as the State is the image of the human being, it is also the image of man (*Mannes*)."[1] That the State is masculine and not feminine is indicated by the contrasted bearing that man and woman respectively assume, by nature, to the State. Man feels himself in his proper character and sphere, "in his full human freedom, in his spiritual mastery (*geistige Herrschaft*)" in the State; woman, on the other hand, has "a certain natural aversion to politics and political activity." Men (*Männer*) form and guide the State. "It is the image of their peculiar nature."[2] It would thus be pernicious to admit women to political privileges in general: the manly character and spirit of the State must not be enervated through the admixture of feminine susceptibility, passion and subtlety.

[1] *Gesammelte Schriften*, p. 284. *Cf.* also p. 25, note (2): "Ich habe in den psychologischen Studien über Stat und Kirche (*Zürich*, 1845) die Männlichkeit des States näher erörtert. Der französische Ausdruck: *L'État c'est l'homme* bedeutet nicht blos: Der Stat ist der Mensch im Groszen, sondern zugleich: Der Stat ist der Mann im Groszen, wie die Kirche die weibliche Natur im Groszen, die Frau, darstellt."

[2] *Lehre vom modernen Stat*, vol. i, p. 233.

CHAPTER IV

THE STATE AND THE SOCIAL ORGANISM

THE several schools of the new science of sociology have all attempted to correlate their subject with some division of the century's expanding field of reorganized natural sciences. The science of biology has been of peculiar influence upon the development of sociological theory. Though the biological method of approach had, before the appearance of nineteenth-century sociology, been followed, with various limitations and qualifications, by philosophers of the State, yet, as has already been said, the idea appeared more commonly in the theory of society than in political philosophy proper. But society itself having been established within the natural, physical world, the State, as an inseparable part, or organic product, of society, may then, like other social elements and derivatives, be subsumed under the same social-physical categories. Thus in sociology the State may be depicted as organic because it is the social organism in a particular aspect; or because the State is of the same nature as the social organism and subject to the same laws; or because it originates with the social organism and passes through a parallel evolution. Or the State may be treated as an integral part of the social organism, as an organ of society, or a system of social organs. Though the first systematic and detailed employment of the biological method was made by Herbert Spencer, Comte had demonstrated at considerable length the connection of sociology with biology as its immediate predecessor in the hierarchy of sciences, and had traced many analogies between the "social" or "collective" and plant and animal organisms. Since Comte's universal scientific system, in which the special relations between biology and sociology were established, the conception of the social organism has been variously elaborated in the writings of such leading sociologists as Spencer, Lilienfeld, Schäffle, Worms and others.[1] And their general biological theories of social origins and social evolution, and of the analogies between society and animal organisms, have been in various ways applied to political conceptions.

I. COMTE

A fundamental feature of the sociological part of Comte's system of Positive Philosophy[2] is his insistence upon the essential relation of sociology, or social physics, to all the natural sciences. Sociology can be studied, he maintains, only in its relation directly to biology and indirectly to the other sciences which in regular series form the presuppositions of biological study. An interpretation of social phenomena and a formulation of social laws must be founded on the laws governing natural phenomena. There are, Comte says, two general objects of all philosophical

---

[1] The organismic conception of society has likewise been maintained by several scientists, notably the zoologist, Oscar Hertwig, in recent writings. *Cf.* his *Die Lehre vom Organismus und ihre Beziehung zur Socialwissenschaft* (1899), a public address delivered before the University of Berlin; and his *Allgemeine Biologie* (1906), pp. 414-423. For a somewhat similar view put forward by an earlier zoologist, *cf.* Gustav Jäger, *Lehrbuch der allgemeinen Biologie* (2 vols., 1871-7), *passim;* and for the qualified organismic theory of an eminent psychologist, *cf.* W. Wundt, *Vorlesungen über Tier- und Menschenseele* (1863), pp. 171 *et seq.*, *System der Philosophie* (1889), pp. 534-545, 596-604, and *Völkerpsychologie* (5 vols., 1900-08), vol. i, pp. 1-24.

[2] *Cours de philosophie positive*, 6 vols., first edition, 1830-42. Citations here are from the fourth edition, by Littré, 1877.

speculation—namely, the study of man and the study of the exterior world; and there are two methods of philosophical exposition according as the starting-point is from the former or latter field of inquiry.[1] The metaphysical and theological schools begin with the philosophy of man and proceed thence to the study of " nature," and thus apply anthropomorphic conceptions in the interpretation of natural phenomena. The order of the positivist thinker is the reverse: beginning with the investigation of the external world, the phenomena of which are simpler and more readily reducible (in our present stage of knowledge) to scientific generalizations, he passes to the consideration of the more complex phenomena of human life. The further his examination of this field extends the more clearly does he detect its dependence upon general laws. He is thus led to the conclusion that the incompleteness and imperfection of his study, as a science, is due to the complexity of the phenomena and to his relatively limited acquaintance with them, rather than to any exceptional or capricious properties.

The dependence of the science of human society upon the physical sciences is a part of Comte's doctrine of " positivism " — as the only scientific method of studying any phenomena, and of his scheme of the " hierarchy of sciences " based on that doctrine. The positive philosophy [2] confines its investigations to " sense-reports "—the only possible objects (outside of one's self) of knowledge; the " positive " being that which is fixed as true on the basis of sense perception.[3] The positive philosophy is thus distinguished from the futile systems of theology and meta-

---

[1] Vol. iii, lecture 40: " Sur l'ensemble de la biologie."

[2] Vol. i, lecture 1: " Considérations générales sur la nature et l'importance de la philosophie positive."

[3] *Cf.* Ward, *Dynamic Sociology,* vol. i, p. 86.

physics, both of which look beyond mere phenomena (the sense reports), the former seeking for the causes, the latter for the inner essence, the substance, of phenomena.   For this positive, or scientific, study of the universe, Comte expounds his system of the hierarchy of the science.[1]   The order is as follows: Mathematics, Astronomy, Physics, Chemistry, Biology, and Sociology.   As we go down the scale they become less general, and more special; less simple, and more complex; and proportionately less productive of grounds for scientific prevision and prediction.   Comte emphasizes the dependence of each science in the series upon all that precede it, and the applicability of its laws to all that succeed it.   The relation of any one of the series to the one succeeding it is that of genus to species.   The laws of astronomy, for example, apply to the phenomena of physics or biology, but its details are less manifold.

The special relations of sociology to the science immediately preceding it in the hierarchy—namely, biology—are treated in detail.[2]   The affiliation of these two sciences is close, for they are both sciences of organized bodies, as distinguished from the *corps bruts*, or inorganic bodies which form the particular objects of the other four sciences.[3]

In sociology the fundamental factors are order and progress, corresponding to organization and life in biology.[4] The interaction between order and progress is emphasized; progress is regarded as the object of order, and order as the indispensable condition of progress,[5] and practical political and sociological conclusions are deduced from this relation.

[1] *Philosophie positive*, vol. i, lecture 2: "Considérations générales sur la hiérarchie des sciences positives."

[2] *Cf.* especially vol. iv, lecture 49.

[3] Vol. i, pp. 69 *et seq.*   *Cf.* G. H. Lewes, *Comte's Philosophy of the Sciences*, pp. 143 *et seq.*

[4] Lewes, *op. cit.*, pp. 251-2.   [5] *Cf.* Ward, *op. cit.*, vol. i, p. 127.

The general science of " Social Physics " is divided into " Social Statics "—the " laws of co-existence," the status, order, of society, and " Social Dynamics "—the laws of progress, the developing movement of society;[1] these correspond to the divisions of biology, namely, anatomy, dealing with organization, and physiology, dealing with life. Social statics[2] has as its field the study of the action and reaction among the various elements of social existence. As in biology, the guiding view here is that of the natural and necessary harmony between an organism and its environment (*milieu*) as the condition of its life.[3] Social Dynamics treats of the development of humanity.[4] This development is subject to invariable laws. " Each of the successive social states is the necessary result of the preceding state and indispensable condition (*moteur*) of the following state."[5]

As civilization advances these laws become " more irresistible and consequently more cognizable," and " accidental influences " become less active.[6] At any stage in the development the social state should be considered " as perfect as the corresponding age of humanity admits, taking into account the correlative system of circumstances under the empire of which its actual evolution is accomplished."[7] The systematic reformation of humanity must accommodate itself to the course of development.[8] It can not reverse or change the direction or character of the progression. It

[1] *Philosophie positive*, vol. iv, pp. 230–1. *Cf.* Ward, *op. cit.*, vol. i, p. 128.

[2] *Philosophie positive*, vol. iv, lecture 50.

[3] *Cf.* vol. iii, pp. 205, 209–210.

[4] Vol. iv, lecture 51: " Lois fondamentales de la dynamique sociale, ou théorie générale du progrès natural de l'humanité."

[5] *Ibid.*, p. 263.

[6] *Ibid.*, pp. 270–1.   [7] *Ibid.*, p. 279.   [8] *Ibid.*, p. 283.

can, through the agencies of reason and foresight, accelerate
the natural development but can pass over no intermediate
stages.   The evolution consists of a fluctuating movement
about a continuous and unchangeable median line of progression.[1]

A fundamental scientific principle of the Social Dynamics
lies in the " law of the three stages " [2]—the theological, the
metaphysical, and the positive.   These are the stages
through which the human intelligence, considered with regard to the individual as well as humanity, passes.   The
process of social evolution in this aspect is the subject of
the major portion of the Social Dynamics, and constitutes
Comte's philosophy of history.[3]   This is an account and explanation of the evolution of humanity, regarded from the
standpoint of the progress of the human mind, and of the
institutions successively in conformity therewith, through
the three stages.   Each stage being traversed through several gradations, Comte's consideration of the corresponding ideas, institutions, and customs—social, religious and
political, forms a long and rather discursive disquisition.
In particular the intellectual history of Western Europe is
reviewed to demonstrate the successive supremacy enjoyed
by these three attitudes of mind, and to trace the progress
from the lowest—the theological, through the intermediate
—the metaphysical, to the highest and final stage—the positive.   In the theological era,[4] which continued until the close
of the thirteenth century, in its three stages of fetishism,
polytheism, and monotheism, the intervention of some su-
pernatural or divine agency, as the cause of all phenomena,
was assumed.   The metaphysical period [5]—from the fourteenth through the eighteenth century, rejected the deistic

---

[1] *Op. cit.*, pp. 285-292.   [2] *Ibid.*, 490 *et seq.*   [3] Vols. v and vi.
[4] Vol. v, lectures 53 and 54.   [5] *Ibid.*, lecture 55.

interpretation and introduced instead " entities " as explanations. The positive stage,[1] beginning with the nineteenth century, though suggested from the earliest times and foreshadowed in the work of Bacon, Galileo, and Descartes, is the present scientific, positive, age. The characteristics of this positive method have been indicated above. The formative elements of this stage have been gradually developing and converging, simultaneously with the decay of the preceding stage. Its realization as a whole can, however, be said to be but just begun.

Having through a long historical survey constituted the " fundamental theory of [social] evolution " so that it is " henceforth as completely demonstrated as any other essential law of natural philosophy," [2] Comte assumes the task of indicating " the direction which it is necessary to impress upon the systematic movement in order to make it exactly correspond to the spontaneous movement." [3] The various elements, now isolated, of the positive life must be brought together and co-ordinated into a new social system. This indispensable co-ordination is to be first intellectual, then moral, and finally political.[4] There must be set up a spiritual authority distinct from and independent of the temporal authority. " In the present stage, philosophical contemplation and labor are more important than political action, in regard to social regeneration, because a basis is the thing wanted." [5] " Human evolution has been characterized throughout by the ever-increasing influence of the speculative over the active life." [6] " The future spiritual power, first basis of a true reorganization, will reside in a class en-

---

[1] Vol. vi, lecture 56.   [2] Vol. vi, p. 434.
[3] *Ibid.*, p. 435.   [4] *Ibid.*, p. 436.
[5] Martineau, *Positive Philosophy of August Comte*, vol. ii, pp. 466-7.
[6] *Philosophie positive*, vol. vi, p. 440.

tirely new, without analogy to any of those which exist, and originally composed of members issuing . . . from all orders of present society, according to their individual qualifications . . . The gradual advent of this salutary corporation will be, moreover, essentially spontaneous, since its social ascendency can result only from the voluntary assent of men's minds to the new doctrines successively elaborated." [1]   The qualification *par excellence* for spiritual authority is " positive capacity." It has functions in relation both to the general body of people—its educational functions, and to the temporal authority. Its educational functions are general and special. Its general educational function is " to inculcate in individuals the knowledge and habits requisite for living in positive society, which is industrial and universally altruistic." [2]   Its special educational function is " to give each individual the particular knowledge and habits which he will need in the career which he has freely chosen." [3]   In relation to the temporal authority its function is to afford the scientific consultation and surveillance necessary to government in conformity to the principles of positive politics. The primary qualification for temporal authority is " industrial capacity." Its function is the immediate direction of action. It is to organize the division of industrial work. " The spiritual authority will take cognizance of the needs of the people, and will seek, according to the principles of positive science, the best means of satisfying these needs. The temporal authority, represented by the chiefs of industry, will put into operation the means discovered by the *savants*." [4]   The spiritual authority is thus to " govern opinions and manners," while

---

[1] *Philosophie positive*, vol. vi, p. 439.

[2] Defourny, *La Sociologie positiviste: Auguste Comte*, p. 191.

[3] *Ibid.*   [4] *Ibid.*, p. 192.

the temporal authority applies itself only to acts (*actes accomplis*).[1]

In conclusion we may note that the organismic character of Comte's interpretation of the nature of society and social forces appears from his frequent recourse in this exposition to analogies between society and a physical organism. Society is called an organism—a " social " or " collective " organism,[2] as distinguished from the individual plant or animal organisms; and the origin and functions of government are held to bear close relation to the organic constitution of society. For society has the essentially organic attribute of " *consensus universel.*" [3] This means a natural and spontaneous harmony of structure and functions, all parts of a complex system working toward a common end, through the action and reaction of these parts upon one another, and their co-operative activity upon the environment.[4] This solidarity and harmonious action, existing in plants, becoming more perfect in animals, attains in the social organism its completest development;[5] society forms the highest stage of organic evolution.[6] Co-operation is the dominating principle of society, though sympathy also—the sentiment of unity—is an active and necessary element; and this principle of co-operation and sympathy, based on the organic nature of society, has a political consequence. For co-operation demands government. The function of government is to maintain the solidarity of society, to keep active the spirit of the whole, the sentiments of unity. The activity of government is thus of a spiritual and moral, as well as material, nature. Government is, however, a natural outgrowth of

[1] *Philosophie positive*, vol. vi, p. 440.
[2] *Cf.* vol. iv, p. 237; vol. vi, p. 712, *etc.*
[3] Vol. iv, p. 235.   [4] *Ibid.*, pp. 242–3.   [5] *Ibid.*, p. 253.
[6] *Cf.* Barth, *Philosophie der Geschichte als Sociologie*, pp. 27–8.

society; it is a result of co-operative action, and not *vice versa*. A social, and consequently a political, subordination arises spontaneously out of the individual dispositions of the co-operating people. These dispositions are, on the one hand, the desire to rule, naturally inherent in the intellectually superior: and, on the other hand, the inclination naturally inherent in the generality of men, to submit themselves to the guidance of others, the intellectually superior.

Further, social progress, like all organic development, is shown to be characterized by an increasing specialization of function, with the concurrent perfecting evolution of corresponding organs.[1] The maladies, finally, of the social organism, social disturbances, are explained as subject to pathological analysis—a scientific method which here, as in biology, takes the place of experimentation as applied in the sciences of inorganic bodies.[2]

2. SPENCER

Between the date of Comte's *Cours de philosophie positive* and the appearance of Herbert Spencer's first writings in the field of sociology new categories had been introduced into the science of biology. Spencer had been a student of this latter science before he turned his attention to social philosophy; and his method and point of view in his sociology is more thoroughly biological than that of any of his predecessors. In his interpretation of the phenomena of society he employs persistently the method of organic analogy and the use of organic terms. Society he regards as a natural being not distinguishable through any essentially new principles from the other objects of the organic

[1] *Philosophie positive*, vol. iv, p. 417.

[2] *Ibid.*, pp. 308–9. For citation of further analogies, *cf.* Towne, *Auffassung der Gesellschaft als Organismus*, pp. 36–39.

sciences. As the nature of the whole is a consequence of, and can be known only from a knowledge of, the nature of its parts, the study of the parts must logically precede the study of the whole. The starting-point in the explanation of society must be with the individual member of society— with the human being, which corresponds to the cell of the plant or animal organism, the cell having been, since Comte's time, established as the original biological unit. The description of society as an organism, the indication in detail of the analogies between society and plant and animal organisms, and the interpretation, on the basis of these analogies, of the origin and development of society, its elements and their nature and functions, its institutions—" domestic," political, and religious—all this is most completely set forth in the *Principles of Sociology* (1878-80).[1] The general explication of society as an organism is to be found in Part II, " The Inductions of Sociology;" to the special application of this analysis to the State and Government, Part V, " Political Institutions," is devoted.

In pointing out the grounds for his application of the term organism to society,[2] Spencer explains, in the first place that society, though made up of a number of discrete units, must yet be regarded as an entity itself. For " it is the permanence of the relations among component parts which constitutes the individuality of a whole as distinguished from the individuality of its parts," [3] and the term society is to be applied, not to all groups of men, but only " where some constancy in the distribution of parts has resulted from settled life." [4] In the second place, in order

---

[1] Citations here are from the Appleton edition of 1885-6, 3 volumes.

[2] See part ii, ch. i: " What is a Society?" and ch. ii: " Society is an Organism."

[3] Part ii, p. 447.   [4] *Ibid.*, p. 448.

to determine what kind of entity society is, it must be discovered what other entity there is the constant relations among
whose parts are " akin to " the constant relations among the
parts of society.   For " between a society and anything else,
the only conceivable resemblance must be one due to parallelism in the arrangement of components." [1]   As to which of
the two " classes of aggregates "—the inorganic or the organic—society can on this basis be likened to, the former
possibility is eliminated at once: " a whole of which the
parts are alive cannot, in its general characters, be like
lifeless wholes." [2]   There is no such incongruity in the idea
of the similarity in structural principle between society and
an individual organism, and we find " reasons for asserting
that the permanent relations among the parts of society are
analogous to the permanent relations among the parts of an
organic body." [3]   Stated generally, attributes common to a
society and an individual organism are as follows: continuous growth through a period of existence, along with this
growth a differentiation of parts, and a corresponding differentiation in the activities of the parts, and, resulting from
this differentiation of structure and function, a mutual dependence in the activities of the parts; furthermore, each is
an aggregate of vital units, the aggregate surviving the successive lives and deaths of the component units.[4]   There may
seem to be an important unlikeness between society and the
individual organism in the discreteness of the former as compared with the concreteness of the latter.   But this apparent contrast loses most of its significance when we consider
that, on the one hand, in the individual organism the truly
living protoplasmic layers are separated and surrounded by
" semi-vital " and " unvital " parts, such as cartilage, tendon,
hair, nails, and horns: and that on the other hand in society

[1] *Op. cit.*   [2] *Ibid.*   [3] *Ibid.*   [4] *Ibid.*, ch. ii.

in addition to the human beings we should regard as parts
the lower animals and the plants, which, in relation
to the existence of human beings, play as essential a role in
society as do the less vital parts of the body in the individual organism. Furthermore, without avoiding recognition of a distinction of this sort, it should still be observed
that, even with the lack of material contiguity between the
parts of society, there is a dynamic continuity effected by the
transmission of the signs of emotions and ideas in oral and
written language. "That mutual dependence of parts
which constitutes organization is thus effectually established.
Though discrete instead of concrete, the social aggregate is
rendered a living whole." [1]

The general phases of similarity between society and the
individual organism having been thus indicated, Spencer takes
each phase in detail and finds this community of nature more
definitely and obviously verified. In the first place, in social growth [2] analogies to individual organic growth are to
be noted: first, increase in mass—the gradual expansion in
the individual from the first germ to the adult, in society
from the small nomadic group to the large nation; second,
the various sizes reached by different aggregates—in the individual organism ranging from the microscopic protozoon
to the gigantic types of vertebrates, in society, from the
Bushmen family or Fuegian tribe to the nation of aggre-
gated millions; third, in the process of augmentation—in
each simple multiplication of units followed or accompanied
by compounding and recompounding of groups of units;
lastly, within each group of units a further multiplication of
units, producing therefore an increase in mass.

In the second place, there is parallelism in the development of structure.[3] Like the individual organism, society,

[1] Part ii, p. 460. [2] *Ibid.*, ch. iii. [3] *Ibid.*, ch. iv.

along with increase in mass, becomes more heterogeneous in structure. In the primitive group of savages all are engaged in similar activities. There comes in the course of time " the first social differentiation "—the differentiation from the rest of a more influential one or few, the rulers. Later follows the differentiation between the occupations of men and those of women, the former assuming primarily regulative and protective functions, the latter, the sustentative functions. There are subsequent additions to this latter class, by the capture of slaves in war and by other sociological agencies; and this is further accompanied by the subdivision within the two primary divisions of the regulative and sustentative groups. A parallelism to be remarked in the process of differentiation is that " differentiations proceed from the general to the more special;" first " large parts " become unlike one another, and then the parts of a given part become unlike one another. Further, in both the individual organism and society there is a " community of structure " among the different organs. For example, in an animal each organ—*e. g.* the viscus, the liver—is unlike the others with respect to more minute structure and general function, yet each has appliances, respectively, for " bringing prepared materials," for " drafting off vitiated materials, and for carrying away effete matters." Likewise in society, be it a " cotton-weaving district," " seaport," or university, each—though unlike the others in more minute details of organization and in general activity — has a similar " general type of structure;" there are in each agencies for bringing in materials, agencies for distributing the product, agencies for control, and agencies for transmitting orders and reports. Lastly, in both the individual organism and society " there is a contrast between the original mode of development and a substituted later mode;" [1] an organ that is formed through long stages in the organic evolution from a low to a high type is formed more directly in the higher type itself. For example, in the development of the embryo of a mammal the liver is formed without passing through the stages of its successive prototypes in the lower orders of animals. Similarly in society, where a manufacturing industry develops in a new locality it assumes at once the present industrial form of organization without first passing through the historical stages of industrial evolution.

In the third place, the functional differentiation accompanying the differentiation in structure under the forms just outlined is subject to the same development in social and in individual growth.[2]

Finally, the increasing mutual dependence of parts with the advance towards higher types is similar in social and individual evolution.[3] In the lowest stages, in each case either there is no structural differentiation or " the parts can assume one another's functions," so that the loss of one part has no harmful effect upon the others. With developing differentiation the loss of any one part becomes increasingly injurious to the other parts and to the whole, and, in the highest type, results fatally. Cut a sponge in two, and each section continues to live and carry on its normal processes; destroy part of a wandering group of savages and those remaining live pretty much as before. On the other hand the effects of cutting off, for example, the coal-mining population from the rest of England, though perhaps not as destructive as would be the mutilation of the living animal organism of the highest type, would be seriously baneful to the rest of the English society.

Spencer's exposition of organic analogies in the origin,

---

[1] Part ii, p. 483.   [2] *Ibid.*, ch. v.   [3] *Ibid.*, pp. 489–490.

development, structure, and functions of the State and government appears both in the discussion of the political order as a particular organic system within the social existence, and in the special analysis further made of political institutions in the part devoted to that subject.[1]   The " regulative system "[2] forms the third of three systems of organs, the other two being, first, the " sustaining system,"[3] under which the industrial system of society is compared to the system of alimentary organs in the individual organism; and, second, the " distributing system "[4]—under which the commercial system of society is compared to the vascular, circulatory system of animal organs.   In the consideration of the regulative system analogies are traced in detail between the political organization of society and the individual nervo-motor system.   The origin of political control, as of the directive, defensive system in animals, is explained to have resulted from the exigencies arising out of the necessities of conflict with aggressive or competing neighbors; and further political evolution, as regards the development of the different elements of government as well as the historical changes in the general character of the constitution, is interpreted as conforming to the evolution of the nervo-motor system of animals.

The origin of society, as distinguished from a mere unorganized group of men, is, Spencer holds, in co-operation.[5] A co-operating group of men constitutes a society.   The motives to co-operation are, in general, the better satisfaction of wants and the alleviation or prevention of injuries. " But co-operation implies organization.   If acts are to be effectively combined, there must be arrangements under which they are adjusted in their times, amounts, and char-

---

[1] Part v.   [2] Part ii, ch. ix.   [3] *Ibid.*, ch. vii.
[4] *Ibid.*, ch. viii.   [5] Part v, ch. ii.

acters." [1]   The social organization is of two kinds—" distinct in their origins and natures." One is entered into spontaneously and more or less unconsciously in the pursuit of private ends. This is the organization by which a division of labor is accomplished. An individual, naturally, of his own initiative, instigated by the desire for his own profit, engages in that particular task which he finds by experience yields him the greater return. The industrial system is thus initiated. In accord with its origin this organization in its development remains predominantly automatic, regulated by the natural adjustment of supply to demand. The other type of organization is consciously initiated with a public end in view. From the necessities of defense of the society, the individual, often against his private interest, but in obedience to the will of society as a whole or of some leading warrior, co-operates with the others in the interest of the common welfare. This characteristic subjection of the individual to the command of superiors in the organization, is maintained throughout the development of this type of organization, the end of which is the security of society.

This latter type of organization is the political. " Political organization is to be understood as that part of social organization which constantly carries on directive and restraining functions for public ends." [2]   "As in the individual organism that nervo-muscular apparatus which carries on conflict with environing organisms, begins with, and is developed by, that conflict; so the government military organization of a society is initiated by, and evolves along with, the warfare between societies. Or to speak more strictly, there is thus evolved that part of its governmental organization which conduces to efficient co-operation against

---

[1] Part v, p. 244.

[2] *Ibid.*, p. 247.   *Cf.* also part i, p. 12, part ii, pp. 556–574.

öther societies." [1]   Investigation has shown that in tribes
so situated that they never come into clash with other tribes
there is no political organization, no political or military
chiefs. [2]   In tribes which circumstances bring into occasional
wars the military leader appears, at first only as a temporary
chief, the subordination indispensable to the prosecution
of war disappearing upon the recurrence of peace.   With
more frequent wars, either of conquest or of defense, the
necessity of some more permanent headship makes itself
felt, the authority of a regular chief becomes an established
custom, and his power grows greater as war, or the possibility of war, becomes more constant.   The regulating system having been thus initiated, there are similar lines of
further development in the individual and the social organism.   In each the evolution is from a relatively small
and little differentiated system for simple aggregates to a
larger and more complex system for compound aggregates.
In the evolution of the compound animal-aggregate there
appears first " a superior co-ordinating centre."   In the
lower *Annulosa* the similar segments have similar nervous
structures; in the higher species—in which these segments
are highly integrated and differentiated—" there arise at the
end which moves foremost, more developed senses and ap-
pendages for action," [3] and this anterior section exercises a
control over the posterior segments.   In the political evolution of a society, where several neighboring tribes unite
for purposes of common defense, there is a compound headship; and with the eventual formation out of such alliances
of a permanent union, the necessity for co-ordination among
the component headships renders indispensable a central
power with control over the other, now subordinate, powers. [4]

[1] Part ii, p. 525.   [2] *Ibid.*, ch. ix.   [3] *Ibid.*, p. 525.
[4] *Ibid.*, p. 523.

In both types of organism this controlling center becomes larger and more complex as the reports to be received and the movements to be impelled become more frequent and varied.

In the vertebrate series, beginning in its lowest members with an almost uniform cord formed of local centres undirected by a brain, we rise finally to a cord appended to an integrated cluster of minor centres through which are issued the commands of certain supreme centres growing out of them. In a society it similarly happens that the political agency which gains predominance, is gradually augmented and complicated by additional functions. The chief of chiefs begins to require helpers in carrying on control. He gathers around him some who get information, some with whom he consults, some who execute his commands. No longer a governing unit, he becomes the nucleus in a cluster of governing units.[1]

Analogous to the cerebrum in man, we have the legislative assembly in political society.[2] The general function of each is that of deliberation, and the object of the activity of each is the general or future, rather than the transitory or immediate interest; ordinary and routine movements being conducted by the automatically acting lower centres. Each receives information and executes its judgments indirectly, the cerebrum through sensory and through motor centres, the legislature through popular petitions, the press, and commissions, and through the ministers and the administrative and judicial offices.[3]

---

[1] Part ii, p. 529.   [2] *Ibid.*, pp. 530-1.

[3] *Cf.* part v, chs. v–ix, for a detailed exposition—from a naturalistic, though not specifically organismic, standpoint—of the origin and development of the " triune political structure " briefly indicated above, namely, " Political Heads " (ch. vi), " Consultative Bodies " (ch. viii), and " Representative Bodies " (ch. ix).

The existence of a distinct controlling centre makes necessary a system of swift communication whereby information may be brought and orders transmitted.[1]   In both the individual and the social organism this system evolves concomitantly with the evolution of the controlling system. Thus in animals the gradual evolution is from the entire absence of the means of transferring impulses, in such lower forms as, for example, sponges, through the slow diffusion of molecular changes in hydrozoa, to the first appearance, in polyzoa, of distinct nerve-fibres along which are more rapidly transmitted the impulses from the likewise first appearing distinct nerve-centres.   A somewhat similar development we may trace in society from the slow and unregulated diffusion of information from person to person in unorganized savage tribes; with the beginnings of conscious co-operation we discover the communicating system of signal fires; and the evolution of the means for the transmission of intelligence may be further followed through the agencies of the messenger, the letter, the " news letter " in its various stages, and, finally, the telegraph.[2]

"In both kinds of organisms the regulating system, during evolution, divides into two systems, to which is finally added a third partially-independent system." [3]   In the individual organism " the external doings must be quick in their changes.   Swift motions, sudden variations of direction, instant stoppages, are needful; " [4] and these are constantly

---

[1] Part ii, pp. 533–538.

[2] Spencer suggests minute analogies in the comparison of the telegraph to the organic nerve fiber.   The clusters of wires emerging from large social centres, diverging and re-diverging into minor clusters correspond to the main and lateral bundles of nerves; there is insulation for each, the non-conducting substance for telegraph wires corresponding to the medullary sheaths for the nerve fibers.

[3] Part ii, p. 538.   [4] *Ibid.*, p. 539.

under the impulsion of the higher nerve centres. On the other hand, the internal activities of sustentation, which largely repeat themselves in all essentials and therefore need no swift adjustments to meet new demands, are almost exclusively co-ordinated by the unconscious agency of the sympathetic system of nerves, the higher centres exercising control only in case of unusual or abnormal occurrences. Corresponding to this sympathetic nervous system in animals, we have, in the social organism, the regulative agencies of the industrial system (prices, credit, banks, *etc.*) in which the regulation is by the more or less automatic action of the relation of supply and demand, and by the reciprocal influence of the various elements of that system. In the more highly developed polities the power, direction, or aid of the government is employed in this sphere only when anomalous conditions require rectification from above. In society, however, the relations with other societies demand a centralized power with ability and authority to co-ordinate the social organs into quick and special adaptations to meet the various occasions for its action. For the individual organism, the " separation of the two functionally-contrasted regulating systems . . . is a concomitant of greater evolution." [1] Likewise in society the evolution has been from an undifferentiated control of industrial and military activities, through various stages of a partly independent industrial system, to the almost wholly self-regulating industrial systems in the more advanced States of the present. We see, among tribes low in the scale of civilization, the hunt for wild-beasts and the combat with hostile tribes carried on under the same organization. Above that stage the gradual movement—up through the feudal polities, in which industry is specially and not entirely regulated by the military

[1] Part ii, p. 541.

government—is ever towards a more complete release of the industrial system from State interference.

From his theory of society and the State as organic in nature and in development, Spencer frequently deduces arguments in support of his views in the field of more practical political science. This is particularly true in connection with his discussion of the proper functions of government. In the *Principles of Ethics* (1879)[1] his theory of the sphere of the State is implicated with his conception of justice.[2] The duties of the State,[3] he here maintains, are derived from the needs of the citizens. The end of the State is to secure as far as possible that relation between conduct and results of conduct, in which each adult " experiences the good and evil results of his own nature and consequent conduct." [4]

The State's duty—and, therefore, authority—to preserve this relation entails upon it two functions. The primary function, which, as has been shown, formed the original motive of political organization, is defense against external aggression, the success of which aggression would destroy this relation. Its secondary function is to prevent internal encroachments, reciprocally among the individuals in the State. For a first condition to the maintenance and furtherance of life in individual and race is that each individual shall receive or suffer the good or evil results of its own nature and consequent actions. In general only so far as this condition is fulfilled can the principle of the " survival of the fittest " have actualization, and upon this principle depends the survival of the species as well as the progressive evolution of the species.[5] This condition is the condition of jus-

---

[1] Citations here are from the Appleton edition of 1892-3, 2 vols.

[2] Part iv.   [3] *Ibid.*, chs. xxv *et seq.*   [4] *Ibid.*, p. 213.

[5] *Ibid.*, pp. 12 *et seq.*, 18-29, 60-61.

tice. It has a positive and a negative aspect. The formula
of justice [1] " must be positive in so far as it asserts for each
that, since he is to receive and suffer the good and evil
results of his actions, he must be allowed to act. And it
must be negative in so far as, by asserting this of every one,
it implies that each can be allowed to act only under the
restraint imposed by the presence of others having like
claims to act." [2]   The formula of justice is thus as follows:
" Every man is free to do that which he wills, provided he
infringe not upon the equal freedom of any other man." [3]

These two classes of necessary functions determine the
limits of the proper activity of the State.[4] Any further
extension tends to impede the natural evolution of the social organism of which the State forms a part. For an essential factor of evolution is, as has been mentioned, an increasing specialization in structure and function. To attempt to maintain a centralization of activity in the government is to hamper this developing specialization—to deprive
the other parts of political society of their normal functions.
When governmental organs undertake to discharge functions not essentially proper to them, they draw sustenance
and energy from the organs to which these functions naturally pertain.

This individualistic opinion as to the sphere of the State
is further based on a distinction between the nature of society and of the individual organism—a distinction already
referred to, namely, that of the " discreteness " of the
former as compared with the " concreteness " of the latter.
For though we saw that Spencer, in the discussion of the
general similarity between the two, sought from one point
of view to minimize the importance of this apparent un-

---

[1] Part iv, ch. vi.   [2] *Ibid.*, p. 45.
[3] *Ibid.*, p. 46.   [4] *Ibid.*, ch. xxvii.

likeness, he nevertheless added that from the discreteness of
society there does result a " contrast of great significance—
a contrast fundamentally affecting our idea of the ends to
be achieved by social life." [1]   In society there is no specialized seat of feeling and thought.   " Though the discreteness of a social organism does not prevent subdivisions of
functions and mutual dependence of parts, yet it does prevent that differentiation by which one part becomes an organ
of feeling and thought, while other parts become insensi-
tive." [2]   In the individual organism the welfare of the
nervous system, as the seat of sentiency, becomes the ultimate object to which the activities of the insentient parts
contribute.   "But while the regulative structures of the social
organism tend, like those of the individual organism, to
become specialized as seats of feeling, the tendency is checked
by want of that physical cohesion which brings fixity of
function; and it is also checked by the continued need for
feeling in the mechanically-working units for the due discharge of their functions." [3]   Feeling being in all the units
of society, the welfare of these units is the object of society.
There being no completely differentiated " social sensorium," the welfare of society apart from that of its units
" is not an end to be sought.   The society exists for the
benefit of its members; not its members for the benefit of
society." [4]

Finally, from the fact of the increasing specialization of
structure which accompanies the development of a society to
a larger, stronger, " higher " type, Spencer derives an argument against any attempted rigidity of social forms, particularly as this rigidity may be manifested in an organization

---

[1] *Principles of Sociology*, part ii, p. 460.   [2] *Ibid.*   [3] *Ibid.*, p. 461.
[4] *Ibid.*, pp. 461-2. For Spencer's more general qualification of his
organismic theory of society, *cf. ibid.*, ch. xii.

whereby positions and occupations are transmitted by heredity.   As growth — whether increase in size or development in type—is always followed by increasing complexity
in structure, so " changeableness of structure is a condition
to further growth . . . Organization in excess of need
prevents the attainment of that larger size and accompanying higher type which might else have arisen." [1]   One essential element of changeableness of the structure of society
is the freedom among the individuals to fill positions and
perform functions according to their personal qualifications.
" The acquirement of function by inheritance conduces to
rigidity of structure, the acquirement of function by efficiency conduces to plasticity of structure. Succession by
descent favors the maintenance of that which exists. Succession by fitness favors transformation, and makes possible
something better." [2]

3.   LILIENFELD

The *Thoughts Concerning the Social Science of the
Future* (1873-1881) [3] of Paul von Lilienfeld, began to appear before the publication of Spencer's *Principles of Sociology*; and though in an indirect way the general influence
of Spencer's earlier expressed biological conceptions of society may have reached Lilienfeld, the work of the latter is
(as pointed out by Barth [4]) undoubtedly to be considered
as primarily independent of that influence. Evidences of
this independence appear both in the details of his argumentation and the method of his organismic analysis. The
German sociologist, furthermore, puts greater stress upon

[1] Part v, pp. 261-2.   [2] *Ibid.*, p. 260.

[3] *Gedanken über die Socialwissenschaft der Zukunft*, 5 vols. Various
points of his sociological system here presented are subsequently treated
in papers published in the *Annales de l'institut de sociologie*.

[4] *Phil. d. Gesch. als Sociol.*, pp. 127-8 and note.

the reality of the organic character of society and the State; the first volume of his general work, referred to above, is entitled—"Human Society as Real Organism."[1] Those who, in discussing the analogies between nature and society and between the natural and the social sciences, conceive these analogies only as rhetorical figures, he regards as involved in futile doctrinairism and "metapolitics" (*Metapolitik*).[2] In order to keep one's self within the domain of reality, of truth, and nature, "one must acquire the conviction that this or that social group, this or that state, is a real, living organism, like all other organisms in nature, which, further, are evolved (*sich entwickeln*) in space and time not ideally only, but really, and which are cognizable as such."[3] The differences between society and plant and animal organisms are only such as to determine the former as a member of a third, and "highest," kingdom in the general realm of organic beings. The author shows the general affinity of society to the other two classes of organisms through a demonstration of the essential similarity in their determinate constituents and properties. But the parallelism is more fully exhibited in the exposition of his theory of social evolution, this being in part a sociological application of Haeckel's statement of the general principles of biological evolution. Lilienfeld's organismic sociology is characterized, finally, by his systematic consideration of "social pathology:" this forms the subject of a special treatise.[4]

---

[1] *Die menschliche Gesellschaft als realer Organismus.*

[2] Vol. i, pp. 26, 28.

[3] *Ibid.*, p. 27. *Cf.* his statement in *Annales*, vol. ii, p. 250: "Nous étudions le système nerveux social et la substance intercellulaire sociale dans le même sens qu'un zoologue et un médecin observent le système nerveux individuel et les substances dont il est nourri."

[4] *La Pathologie sociale*, 1896.

If we regard the attributes which distinguish organic from inorganic, or the action of organic forces from that of inorganic forces,[1] we shall find, Lilienfeld holds, that each of these attributes pertains to human society " in a higher degree." The primary characteristic of the organism consists in "the more intense and varied interaction of forces." The particular sort of inner vibrations which determines the nature of any given inorganic body remains always the same; inorganic forces repeat the same motions. Organic forces run through a cycle of movements, differing in successive periods of time, though following each other in a definite and causal connection. In human society the difference in this respect from a natural organism is only one of degree; there is a greater diversity and heterogeneity of movements; society is " a more many-sidedly developed organism, in which purposivity (*Zweckmässigkeit*), spirituality (*Geistigkeit*), and freedom prevail over causation, materiality, and necessity in a higher degree than in all other organisms of nature." [2]

Related to this distinction is, secondly, that respecting the inner unity of an organism.[3] The unity of an inorganic body consists in the cohesive attraction of an aggregation of particles tending towards one centre of gravity—in the resistance which the body offers to forces from without tending to destroy its integrity or change its contour.[4] Organic unity consists in a definite causal interaction of forces; it is the coherence and continuity of movements successively changing: here the inner interaction of forces results not in one stable form, but in a series of forms following each

[1] *Gedanken*, vol. i, ch. vii: " Unterschied in der Wirkung unorganischer und organischer Kräfte."

[2] *Gedanken*, vol. i, pp. 57-8.   [3] *Ibid.*, p. 58.

[4] *Cf. Annales*, vol. ii, pp. 246-7.

other in essential connection with each other. "Human society forms the highest unity of all organic bodies; in it the purposivity of movements, the variability (*Beweglichkeit*) of forms, the independence of particular parts remaining in constant and consequent (*consequenter*) subordination to the same general principle, attain a higher stage."[1]

This purposivity (*Zweckmässigkeit*) of the action of matter and force constitutes a third characteristic of organisms.[2] The stone falls to the earth, the magnet draws the iron, without aim; the action of the forces has no apparent relation to the continued existence of the bodies. Even in the lowest organisms, on the other hand, there is an end to be attained in all their organic movements; the plant in absorbing chemicals from the earth thereby maintains its life and growth. In the higher organisms this purposefulness is too evident to need illustration, especially as it appears in the personal consciousness, reason, and will of the human being. In society it has its highest manifestation; a social action is never aimless. Here "personal consciousness, personal reason, personal will, appear as social consciousness, as general human reason, as social freedom; the latter can have for society an inner or outer significance according as the activity of society limits itself to the interaction of individuals, or is directed against the forces of nature or of other social units."[3]

In the fourth place, organic bodies are characterized by their structural perfectibility (*Vervollkomnung*).[4] This consists in the gradually increasing specialization of inner and outer parts and of the functions pertaining thereto, the specialization coming about in connection with the successive accommodations of the organism to its environment,

[1] *Gedanken*, vol. i, p. 58.

[2] *Ibid.*, pp. 58–61.

[3] *Ibid.*, p. 61.

[4] *Ibid.*, pp. 61–64.

in repelling noxious forces and appropriating beneficial substances. Here again the characteristic appears most completely in human society.

The inner and outer specialization of organs, the inner and outer morphological and physiological organization (*Gliederung*) . . . pertains also to human society, only in a relatively higher degree. Every organization, every form, every configuration, is conditioned by differences in the limitation of movement (*wird durch Unterschiede in der Begrenzung der Bewegung bedingt*), and since human society manifests the most many-sided, varied, and purposeful movements, it follows that human society must present the most developed organization and organic specialization.[1]

Finally, capitalization (*Kapitalisirung*)[2]—the storing up of energies and materials for future consumption—is a distinctly organic function, and is most operative in society. And in the latter, as in natural organisms, the capitalization may be either in the form of an amassing of exterior objects, or of an internal accumulation and transformation of materials and forces.

The outer capitalization of natural forces in human society manifests itself in the most varied aspects and forms, depending upon the stage of development of the society. Buildings, supplies, instruments, money, improvements of every sort—in short, everything which is applied by man not to the immediate satisfaction of his needs, but to the bringing forth of other goods, or everything the use of which he postpones in time or distributes in space, with the object of using it at the appropriate time and place—all that constitutes only various forms of capital.[3]

But " human society, as organism, represents not only a

[1]*Gedanken*, vol. i, pp. 63-4.   [2]*Ibid.*, pp. 64-8.   [3]*Ibid.*, pp. 65-6.

higher outer, but also a greater inner, capitalization of forces. Through social life are capitalized not only exchange values, but also personal goods." [1]

Thus human society has the five essential attributes of an organism, and each in a higher and more completely developed form. It is an error to object that other organisms appear in definite forms, whereas society consists of a combination of elements which do not interact within fixed limits.[2] For the conception of corporeal individuality is only relative; it denotes more or less concentration of forces within certain limits. Furthermore, the configuration of a natural living body is never absolutely fixed; the form of plant or animal is not unchanging. The higher degree of automatic activity and self-determination of the cell-individuals of the social organism, as compared with the parts of which other organisms are composed, is a sign of the higher development of society as an organism.[3] Nor can the fact that society as a whole is not apprehensible by human perception be taken as evidence that it has not an integral reality. From separate perceptions of parts of the earth's surface, of mountains, plains, bodies of water, we attain, through rational imagination, a conception of the earth as a real unit; so from traditions, historic remains, descriptions, and personal observations, one forms a more or less true image of the social structure, the social development, of this or that society, of this or that nation or State, although no man is in a position to comprehend all such activities and events into a whole perceivable by the senses.[4]

Social organisms thus constitute, with animals and plants, a third kingdom within the organic realm. The essential difference (apart from the higher degree of development

---

[1] *Gedanken*, vol. i, p. 68.   [2] *Ibid.*, pp. 140 *et seq.*
[3] *Ibid.*, p. 141.   [4] *Ibid.*, p. 148.

manifested in all its organic attributes, and apart from a distinction in its composition indicated below) of the social from the other two types lies in the autonomous mobility of its parts.[1]   In the plant kingdom neither the individual nor its parts are capable of autonomous movement; in the animal kingdom, the individual, but not its parts, moves autonomously; in the social kingdom, both the " unified aggregate " — a social organism, and its " anatomical elements "—men or groups of men, are endowed with power of autonomous movement.[2]

The social organism is made up of cellular substance (social cells and tissues) and intercellular substance.[3]   The cells of society are the individual nervous systems of men.[4] That is, with Lilienfeld individual man forms the cell of society only to the extent of his nervous system, not, as with Spencer, " with all his physical attributes." [5]   The social tissues are the various groupings of men in classes, professions, and corporations.[6]   The superior position occupied by society in the organic scale consists in the fact that it is composed of " no other cells but nerve cells, and no other tissues but nerve tissues." [7]   These constitute the primary element of the social organism.[8]   The secondary

---

[1] *Annales*, vol. iii, pp. 134-5.

[2] *Ibid.*, vol. ii, p. 248: " Mais ce n'est que par la société humaine que la nature réalise dans sa plénitude le degré le plus élevé de la vie organique: l'autonomie dans les parties et dans l'ensemble du même organisme individuel."

[3] *Gedanken*, vol. ii, ch. iv.   [4] *Ibid.*, vol. i, p. 139.

[5] *Cf.* Barth, *op. cit.*, pp. 129-130.   [6] *Gedanken*, vol. iii, p. xi.

[7] *Ibid. Cf. Annales*, vol. ii, p. 243.

[8] It is foolish, Lilienfeld asserts, to assume that society, because it is an organism, must possess organs analogous to the head, eye, ear, *etc.*, of a natural organism.   It is true, functions which these organs fulfill for the animal may be performed by organs of society: but within

element is the intercellular substance—broadly, the entire medium in which man works: on the one hand, the earth and its products, the water and the air and their inhabitants; on the other hand, the transformations in that medium which result from man's reactions upon his environment. In a narrower sense social intercellular substance denotes the objects of value to man the utilities of which have been created through the work of saving of man. But since capital and labor are nothing except the collection and adaptation of natural forces for human ends, and since nature is accessible to man only through some sort of human labor—physical or spiritual, conscious or unconscious—an absolute division between natural environment as a whole and that part of it that has been made socially useful through human agency, or between intercellular substance in the broader and in the narrower sense, is not possible.[1] But the social intercellular substance consists (as appears from the author's further development of the conception) not only of the physical medium—both natural and as modified by man—in which the social cells exist, but also of all the means and institutions, of whatever character, that associated men have established as social agencies. In other words, " as social intercellular substance is classed everything which, though outside of the living men, yet exists in society, therefore all which man has appropriated or produced " [2]—buildings, machines and factories, streets

---

a society there exist no organs respectively confined to these specific functions. An Academy of Art, for example, in relation to pictorial and plastic art, may act as a social organ of sight, in relation to music and poetry, as a social organ of hearing. *Cf. Zur Vertheidigung der organischen Methode in der Sociologie*, pp. 54 *et seq.*, and Towne, *op. cit.*, p. 54.

[1] *Gedanken*, vol. ii, pp. 98–9.   [2] Barth, *op. cit.*, p. 130.

and telegraphs, customs, laws, books, works of art, language, ideas.[1]

"The government is the brain of the social aggregate;" it is the highest socially unifying organ and the highest representative of the social consciousness. "Every community of men presents . . . three spheres: the economic, judicial, and political, which correspond, respectively, to the physiological, morphological, and unitary spheres of the organisms of nature."[2]   In other words, as there exists no physical organism without physiological activity, morphological delimitation, and unity, so every human society in some way provides for the needs of the group (economic activity), mutually delimits—through customs and laws—the actions of the individuals (juridical activity), and in some way co-ordinates and unifies the interests and tendencies of the individuals.[3] The political sphere of social life thus represents the general unification — through a "hierarchization" — of the social forces.[4] The unifying tendencies manifest themselves in the hierarchic construction of each of the composite parts of a social aggregate or of an organism of nature, as well as in the organic social or individual whole itself.[5] Each subordinate form of association—the family, the industrial corporation—has a centralized organization; social and industrial classes are superimposed upon one another in hierarchic order; and these several organs and elementary groups are further co-ordinated and stratified into a unified whole. "These different modes of social organization, as also the government

[1] *Gedanken*, vol. ii, pp. 118, 134-5, *etc.*; *Pathologie Sociale*, p. 138. Lilienfeld discusses the social intercellular substance at greater length and in greater detail than the social cellular substance.

[2] *Pathologie*, p. xxix; *Gedanken*, vol. i, pp. 81-92, 116-119; vol. ii, p. 77, *etc.*

[3] *Cf. Annales*, vol. ii, p. 240.   [4] *Ibid.*   [5] *Ibid.*, vol. ii, p. 238.

and all its organs, belong to the political sphere of social
life, in so far as they realize the principle of hierarchy." [1]

The place of the government in the social organism is
thus determined by its character as central and highest organ
of these unifying forces in so far as they are socially conscious and voluntary forces. The unifying, inter-co-or-
dinating forces in the social aggregate are as such political,
but are not all governmental. Not all unifying tendencies
are consciously (from the standpoint of social consciousness) and centrally directed. " Governmental forms, properly speaking, ... express only the construction of the
central organ which represents the supreme unity of action of the social nervous system." The government is thus
" the brain of the social aggregate." [2] As the nervous system of man consists in a sum of organs each of which possesses more or less self-activity,—in other words, each is a
centre of the conscious, subconscious, or half-conscious nervous reflex—so " society represents just such a sum of more
or less conscious or unconscious wills." [3] In society the
wills of all the individuals interact according to the same
laws that govern the interaction of the nerve cells, fibres,
and centres in each animal organism. The principle of the
unconscious has the same significance here as in any other
organism. The individually conscious activity of each particular human being is no conscious activity from the standpoint of society as a whole. As in man only a small part of
his inner and outer activities and only certain elements of
his physical and spiritual development are accompanied by
consciousness, so in society only a limited number of individual acts, only the more important events, only the more
eminent personalities enter into the consciousness of the

---

[1] *Cf. Annales*, p. 239.   [2] *Ibid.*, pp. 237–8.

[3] *Gedanken*, vol. i, pp. 186–7.

whole society as an organic unit. The "highest representative" of this social consciousness is the government (*Regierung*).

The government, as the sovereign power, as the incorporation of social unity, takes up into itself the wills of the individual members of society and reflects back upon them the collective will, directly or through the agency of various intermediate organs. But the government . . . can receive only a small part of the whole sum of reflexes which are going on among the individual wills traversing the organism. The more highly developed the society is, the more variously, and with the greater fulness, does the government receive the reflexes from all parts of the organism, and therefore the more actively and effectively does it react upon the parts.[1]

The political form — monarchic, democratic, *etc.* — of a society determines the type according to which the community constitutes itself to the end of forming a unity.[2] It is " the expression of the relative co-ordination and hierarchic superposition of the morphological elements and organs " of the social aggregate.[3] The particular type determines the individuality of the social aggregate and has no relation to the degree of development of the latter.[4] It serves to distinguish politically different societies in the same general stage of evolution; just as with animals the same degrees of this hierarchic structural superposition are found among genera occupying different stages of evolution determined by the relative integration of action and differentiation of forces. Thus we find monarchies, hereditary and elective, and republics, aristocratic, oligarchic and democratic, among savage tribes as well as among nations the most ad-

[1] *Gedanken*, vol. i, p. 187. *Cf.* vol. iii, pp. 336-7.

[2] *Annales*, vol. ii, p. 240.   [3] *Ibid.*, p. 241.   [4] *Ibid.*, p. 249.

vanced in civilization and in political organization, as interpreted below.[1]

The political significance of Lilienfeld's conception of the
organic nature of society appears further in his exposition
of the " law of the progressive evolution of society conceived as real organism." [2]   The general law of natural evolution is stated as " progressive integration, accompanied by
differentiation constantly more specialized, of inorganic and
organic forces;" [3] as applied to organisms this signifies an
" increasing hierarchic concentration and differentiation, accompanied by a constantly intenser and freer action, of vital
forces " [4] The development of society may be stated for the
three before-mentioned spheres separately, and compared to
the corresponding sides of the growth of a physical organism.[5]   Thus economic development signifies augmentation
of property accompanied by extension of economic freedom, or, expressed in physiological terms, " a greater abund-
ance of nutritive substances accompanied by an intenser
physiological action;" juridical development means a clearer
and more detailed definition of individual and common
rights, accompanied by greater freedom in the enjoyment,
and greater security in the assertion, of those rights; as
morphological development means " a more developed differentiation of organs accompanied by their more varied
interaction with each other and the whole." Political development means a stronger united and authoritative action
accompanied by an extension of political liberties; as the
unitary development of an individual organism is towards

---

[1] *Annales*, vol. ii, pp. 235–240.

[2] The author's more succinct statement of this law is in the *Introduction* of the *Pathologie sociale*, pp. xxix, *et seq.*

[3] *Ibid.*, p. xxx.   [4] *Annales*, vol. ii, p. 247.

[5] *Cf. ibid.*, pp. 251 *et seq.; Gedanken*, vol. ii, pp. 337 *et seq.*

" an intenser concentration of forces combined with greater independence of the parts."

History and observation afford practical verification of these laws of social evolution. In an economic contest between two societies, that society will triumph which has, *cæteris paribus*, the greater capital; or which, *cæteris paribus*, enjoys the greater liberty in the production and exchange of wealth. The State which has the stronger central authority, or in which political liberties are more widely exercised, will in either case, other things being equal, triumph, in case of conflict, over the State in which the central authority is weak or political freedom is restricted. Evolution in any given society, as in a natural organism, may embrace all three spheres concurrently, or may manifest itself pre-eminently in only one, for a particular period of time, and be accompanied by comparative stability or even retrogression in either or both of the other spheres. Political decay, for example, may be the concomitant of economic progress.[1]

Interpreting more broadly the features of political evolution, higher integration of forces here may be said to consist in

the more effectual subordination of the lower to the higher, of the particular to the general, considered from the standpoint of the personality of man. Influence, power, *etc.*, if they are the result of a superior and more forceful personality, or of the combination of political rights, privileges, *etc.*, in the hands of particular individuals or classes, represent the integration of political forces in the social nerve-system. This political integration is likewise manifest in the intercellular substance—the objects of value circulating in the State—in the application of a greater portion of these objects to general

[1] *Pathologie*, pp. xxxvii–xxxix.

ends, through the mediation and authority of the State. The differentiation of forces in the political cellular substance finds expression in the greater political independence and freedom of the individual and of social groups, in their relation to the State; and, in the intercellular substance, in this independence specifically as regards the production, distribution, and enjoyment of the various objects of value, as opposed to the rights and claims of the State and its fiscus.[1]

Finally, certain social therapeutical functions pertain to the organs of government. As the social organism is a real organism it is subject, Lilienfeld holds, to sickness and decay; and his work, *La Pathologie sociale*, is devoted to a diagnosis of the diseases of society and to a social therapeutics. The maladies which afflict the social organism are manifested primarily in the cellular substance—the social nervous system, and indirectly in the disorders in the intercellular substance resulting therefrom. The source of any social disease lies in some improper alteration in the cells, in the form of derangement in place (*heterotopie*), in time (*heterochronie*), or mass (*heterometrie*).[2]

"As every individual malady proceeds from a pathological state of the cell, likewise every social malady has its source in a degeneration or abnormal action of the individual—which constitutes the elementary anatomical unit of the social organism . . . The pathological state consists only in that an individual or group of individuals manifests an activity which is mistimed, or is ill placed, or displays excessive excitation or a lack of energy."[3] In general social diseases of either of the three kinds result ultimately in some sort of *heterometrie*, that is, in some form of super-excrescence in one part and debilitation in another; the most

[1] *Gedanken*, vol. ii, p. 339.   [2] *Pathologie*, p. 21.
[3] *Ibid.*, p. 24.

common infection that society suffers is "parasitism."
"Political parasitism is represented by all those who . . .
do not respond to the demands of their political and official
position, by all those political agitators who have in view
only their personal ambition and interest. A government
which creates sinecures or charges the budget with the maintenance of an excessive number of employees only multiplies
such parasites." [1]   It is the function of the statesman in each
case to discover and apply the remedy appropriate to the
particular malady,[2] to regulate the vital energies of the social organism or to stimulate into action latent social forces.
The therapeutic work of the government, with regard to social anomalies of any kind—economic, juridical, or political
—is always, in the last analysis, that of either checking
overexcitation of some parts, or stimulating other parts in a
state of depression.[3]   Taking again the case of parasitism:
" in countries where the death penalty is not yet abolished,
the most dangerous parasites . . . are exterminated, in like
manner as are the pathogenetic bacilli which infect our
body.   But in all other cases of parasitism . . . it is still to
a process of excitation and depression that society must
have recourse in order to restrain the exploitation of some
elements by others.   By protecting and encouraging individuals and groups too weak to resist such exploitation, at the
same time checking or repressing the parasitic forces, the
regulative organs tend to restore equilibrium." [4]

[1] *Pathologie*, p. 48. Lilienfeld gives no interpretation of the specific
cause of the final old-age decrepitude and the death of the social organism; he holds, however, that the most distinctive symptom of such a
period of decay appears when the constitution and movement of society
assume a less organic, more mechanical character.

[2] *Pathologie*, ch. vii: " Le médecin et l'homme d'Etat."

[3] *Ibid.*, ch. viii, pp. 228 *et seq.*   [4] *Ibid.*, pp. 278-9.

4. SCHÄFFLE

Albert Schäffle in his *Structure and Life of the Social Body* [1] employs the terminology and classifications of biology with a completeness of detail equal to that of Spencer or Lilienfeld. Organismic conceptions are applied throughout his explication of the constitution of society, its origin, development, institutions, and activities. Yet Schäffle maintains that he does not entertain the idea that society is an organism in any sense, of either a higher or lower type. In the preface to the second edition of the above-mentioned work, he asserts that the distinction of this from the former edition lies in the restricted space given to the anthropological and psychological foundations of his system, and in the elimination of many of the biological analogies; but that this abridgment is for the sake of brevity, however, the work having undergone no essential modifications in principle or method. He goes on to say that the first edition nowhere adopted the conception of the organic for the social; but it

conceived the body of society as a life-union (*Lebens-Zusammenhang*)—spiritually, not physiologically, constituted, which stands above organic and inorganic existence. That real analogies not only exist but—because of the sameness of environment for the organic and the social world, and because of the social utilization of the materials and forces of the former—can not fail to exist, is obvious; the indication of such analogies is therefore . . . important for a comprehensive conception of the world. It would have been unwarrantable to have assumed something in the social world which pertains to the phenomena of organic nature only, and to have disregarded the much new which appears in the social world,

---

[1] *Bau und Leben des socialen Körpers;* first edition, 1875-8, 4 vols. Citations here are from the two-volume edition of 1896.

because it was not to be observed in the sphere of organic phenomena. But this double error cannot be imputed to the first edition. An unprejudiced examination of both editions must prove to the reader that such magnificent nonsense—as that attributed to the book by a recent address, in which it was said that one might as well speak of the *Bau und Leben* of the Pandects as of that of the social body—did not at least emanate from the head of the author.[1]

Schäffle calls attention to the more spiritual character of social phenomena, as compared with all other orders of existence; to their far greater modifiability, which (as with Comte) increases with development in complexity of social structure; and to the resulting superior consequence of voluntary, conscious, activity in society.[2] The significance of freedom and consciousness in society does not (as with Lilienfeld) merely render society a higher organic realm, but differentiates it as a domain distinct from the domain of animal and vegetable organisms.

Notwithstanding this implied criticism of the theories which attempt to classify society within the realm of organisms, and which overlook the new and distinguishing elements and properties which society presents, the method of Schäffle's sociology is principally biological. His point of departure is his argumentation that the same laws govern all phenomena—inorganic, organic, and social. Moreover, the close analogies between society and the organism, in structure and action, constitute for him the rational justification for the constant demonstration of those analogies;

[1] *Op. cit.*, vol. i, pp. iv-v.

[2] *Ibid.*, vol. i, pp. 264-5: " Erst im socialen Körper tritt mit der Politik die bewusste Einflussnahme des ganzen Volkskörpers auf die entwicklungsgeschichtlichen und pathologischen Veränderungen der Vitalitätsgrenzen auf."

and he considers that the application of biological categories to the interpretation of the nature and development of society is the most convenient and enlightening method of sociological analysis.   Furthermore, in the execution of this plan, political institutions are taken up by Schäffle in relatively greater detail than by any other sociologist of the organismic school.

In the discussion of the " social body " in " its general relation to the organic and inorganic world," [1] Schäffle maintains that the superficial classification of " the bodies and movements of the earth " into " the inorganic, the organic (plant-animal) and the personal-social worlds " must not obscure the facts of their interrelations and similarities. They are all subject to constant and essential interaction and interdependence; the existence of each is dependent upon the extra-terrestrial world; and there are attributes common to inorganic object, plant, animal, and social body.   In the first place, the elementary stuff and forces of the social body are derived directly from the organic world; and the commodities and forces that are the indispensable auxiliaries to its existence and action, it draws from the inorganic and organic domains.   The plant transformations of chemical substances, effected only in the light and heat of the sun, form nourishment for man; and man is the ultimate element of the social body, which is thus always dependent upon a preliminary organic modification of inorganic materials.   The social body, secondly, can not be distinguished from the inorganic and organic realms as " community from non-community."   " Interaction of all parts of a system of relatively independent unities . . . pervades all domains of empirical manifestation." [2]   This applies to individual organic bodies—each of which is a " life-community of mil-

[1] Vol. i, bk. i, sec. 3.   [2] *Ibid.*, p. 9.

lions of cells "—as well as to inorganic bodies, in which such
forces as chemical affinity and cohesion effect the combinations.   Moreover, the dynamic association of all objects,
however distantly separated in space, is manifested in the
phenomena of gravity, light and heat.   Thirdly, it is incorrect to distinguish the social body " as the bearer of richest
life," from " dead nature." [1]   The vortex of atomic rota-
tions and vibrations in inorganic matter is a lower form of
that equilibration between inner states and outer conditions
which constitutes the life of organic bodies, and of the historical social equilibrations between national types and their
cultural and physical environment.   In the fourth place, the
view that regards the inorganic world as non-psychic (*un-
beseelt*), the organic world as partly psychic (*teilweise beseelt*), falls far short of the truth.[2]   The association of persons in the social body is indeed maintained through such
intellectual means as language and the various institutions
for the dissemination of ideas.   But reason, as present in
the individual man, is a development from the psychic life
(*Seelenleben*) of lower animals, an evolution which may be
further traced continuously back to the primordial irritabil-
ity of the protozoon—or even to the attractive and repulsive
movement of atoms, which is conceived by some as a kind
of sensibility.

The structure and life of the social body are thus distinct
not in essence, but only in degree, from the material systems
and forms of motion of inorganic and organic nature.[3]
There is throughout its whole organization and activity
an adaptation between its organs and the surrounding conditions.   " Wherever one casts one's eye, the social body appears as an *ensemble* of inorganic and of spirit-endowed
(*begeisteten*) masses, of physical, psycho-physical, and psy-

[1] Vol. i, bk. 1, sec. 3, p. 10.   [2] *Ibid.*, p. 11.   [3] *Ibid.*, p. 12.

chic movements, the correlates of which are to be found in the pre-social realms of existence and activity." [1]   When the summit of scientific knowledge shall have been attained " the most complex social phenomena of the world of experience will admit of being comprehended—with the phenomena of evolution, dissolution, equilibration, and rhythm, and the other fundamental phenomena of the organic and inorganic life of nature—under one highest and final law of experience, and not in a mere metaphorical, but in a completely real, sense." [2]   Such an all-embracing law is yet impossible because our knowledge of the social, as well as of the organic and inorganic, realms, still falls so far short of the necessary completeness.   But the foregoing considerations show sufficiently " that every attempt to define the nature and essence of the social body through abstract contrasts with the facts of the inorganic, organic, and individual-psychological existence, is entirely impracticable because there is in last analysis an essential kinship (*Wesens-verwandtschaft*) between the social and the non-social, phenomenal world (*Erscheinungswelt*) and between their respective components." [3]   The social body " takes up into itself all human, animal, vegetable, and inorganic materials and forms of movement of the whole earth-body, comprehends them into one historical life-community, and leads them toward the last, most universal, and most many-sided equilibrium of human spiritual and bodily development with all the external influences of our planet.   The universality and high-degreed spiritualization of its stuff and its movements are the distinctive characteristics of the social body." [4]

---

[1] Vol. i, bk. i, sec. 3, pp. 12-13.   [2] *Ibid.*, p. 14.   [3] *Ibid.*

[4] *Ibid.*, p. 15.   Schäffle's summary definition of " social life " can not be adequately rendered in English: " Das sociale Leben ist die geistigste und universellste Integration, Differentiation und Gliederung

The place of society in the world of phenomena is thus established by Schäffle as the highest of three stages of a universal and continuous evolution of forms and functions. But the author's detailed analysis of the constitution and action of the social body is presented not under general categories, but under the special categories of the next lower stage—the organic. The general study of the forms and functions of society comprise thus : (1) a "social morphology" and a " social physiology," under which are considered the social elements—the individual human being (the active element) and the " national possessions " (*Volksvermögen,* the passive element)—and the combination of these elements into social tissues and organs ; [1] and (2) a " social psychology," under which is examined the " social spiritual-life " (*Das sociale Geistleben*) in its development, phases, and means of expression. [2]

There are five general types of social tissues [3]—each fulfilling some principal social function, each performing a distinct sort of social activity which unites persons and things for some social purpose. There are, in the first place, the " arrangements of domiciliation " (*Niederlassung*) [4]—the *ensemble* of the spatial means of social residence and communication, manifested in buildings, roads, streets, *etc.* (*Gebäuden, Wegen und Stegen, Bodenmeliorationen*). To this social tissue the author indicates no homologue in the

---

aller anorganischen und organischen, aller physischen und psychischen Kräfte der irdischen Welt, die vollkommene Belebung, die vollständigste und bewusste Individuierung, hiemit aber das umfassendste und vergeistigste Gegenbild sowohl der ursprünglichen individualitätslosen Einheit des anorganischen Naturreichs, als der nur stückweisen und halbbewussten Individuation des organischen Naturreichs."

[1] *Ibid.,* vol. i, bks. ii and iv.   [2] *Ibid.,* bk. v.

[3] *Ibid.,* pp. 111–124.

[4] *Ibid.,* pp. 111–112.

animal organism. Secondly, there are the protective tissues (*die socialen Schutzgewebe*).[1] These include the social protective contrivances of all kinds—clothing, roofs, money-safes, fortresses, the army, the police, insurance companies. They are analogous to the epidermal tissue of animals. Thirdly, the economic, or household arrangements (*ökonomische Grundanstalten*),[2] by which is meant the economic and financial organization of the family, and of social, religious, cultural, and political life. Their functions include " the indrawing, consumption, and storing-up of useful material in all tissue parts, . . . what organic physiology calls tissue-nourishment (in distinction from the metabolizing functions of digestion and circulation)."[3] Fourthly, the technical, or practical, social arrangements (*Geschäfts- und Machtanstalten, Kunsteinrichtungen*),[4] comprising the various means for the generation and application of social power in all domains of society. They correspond to the muscular tissues of the animal organism, and appear in two general forms, namely: the means of power, execution,—chiefly represented by the army, police, and state officials; and the means of business administration—chiefly represented by the organs of production and trade. The former are analogous to the cross-striped (*quergestreiften*), or voluntary, muscles; the latter, to the smooth (*glatten*), or involuntary, muscles. Finally, there are the " psycho-physical social tissues "—the institutions of intellectual activity (*die psychophysichen Socialgewebe*),[5] composed of all social ar-

---

[1] *Op. cit.*, pp. 112-114.   [2] *Ibid.*, pp. 114-117.

[3] " Der Haushalt umschliesst nur die Akte des Einkommensbezuges, der Konsumption und der Ausscheidung der Güterstoffe in allen Gewebebezirken, dasjenige was die organische Physiologie Gewebeernährung (im Gegensatz zu den progressiven Stoffwechsel-Hauptfunktionen der Verdauung und des Umlaufes)nennt." P. 114.

[4] *Ibid.*, pp. 117-121.   [5] *Ibid.*, pp. 122-131.

rangements exercising functions of intelligent direction.
They correspond to the nerve-tissues of animals.   The
agencies of public—*i. e.*, political—control form one element
of this system; the arrangements for direction in private
activity—in industry, scientific investigation, schools, *etc.*,
—form parts.   Every social activity in which the intellectual character predominates forms part of the functioning
of the system of social nerve-tissues.

The social organs are variously constituted of tissues of
these five kinds,[1] and may be classed into three main groups:
first, the institutions of the outer national life—of production, trade, transportation, and protection; second, the institutions of the inner national life—of sociality, education
and culture, science, literature and art, and religion; and,
third, " the principal institution of the united will and action
of the entire outer and inner national life—the State and
the commonwealth." [2]

The State comprises the central—the controlling and co-
ordinating, organs of the social nervous-system, together
with the auxiliary organs that protect, support, or serve
them.   The fourteenth book [3] of the *Bau und Leben* is devoted to the exposition of the histology, organology, genesis,
and developmental stages, of the State.

In the State is represented the unity of will and action of
the people of a society as a whole, in so far as the object of
will or action is the perpetuation or other interest of the
whole people.   In the State are comprised the central organs of social will and social power.   Not all manifestations
of the social will are accomplished, or even initiated, by the
central organs.   Some social movements " are regularly
free from all positive and direct influence of the central

---

[1] *Ibid.*, pp. 157–175.

[2] *Ibid.*, p. 175; vol. ii, p. 95.   [3] Vol. ii., pp. 427–591.

stimulating and restraining centres." [1] As in the animal
organism, so in society, the majority of actions are reflex
or sub-conscious movements without any interference by the
central organs. The central organs in such cases have a
potentially checking or co-ordinating function, and participate only when such a restraint or adjustment is necessary
in the interest of the whole. Some social movements, again,
are subject only to a modifying influence by the central organs—"which here act as apparatus of modification, co-
ordination, restraint, and accommodation." [2] Here the control exercised by the central organs is actual, not potential
merely. Finally, there are some social movements which
are conceived, or conceived and executed, wholly by the central organs. [3] These may take the form first of laws, or-
dinances, and decrees set as rules of action for the people
or for the officers of administration; second, of acts performed directly by the central organs through the mandatories of their authority and power. The State is thus " the
regulative central apparatus for co-ordinating all the elements of the general social activity, and the organ of positive interference for preserving the social aggregate. Its
task is the centralized integration of all social will and action in the interest of the maintenance of the whole and of
all the essential parts thereof. In the central universal
corporation—the State— the whole nation attains unity and
individuality." [4]

[1] *Op. cit.*, p. 428.   [2] *Ibid*.   [3] *Ibid*.

[4] *Ibid*.: " Dagegen ist der Staat regulativer Centralapparat der Koor-
dination aller Teile der socialen Gesamtbewegung und Organ des posi-
tiven Eingriffes im Interesse der Gesamterhaltung. Seine Aufgabe ist
einheitliche Integration alles socialen Wollens und Handelns im Interesse
der Erhaltung des Ganzen und alles wesentlichen Glieder des letzteren.
In der centralen Universalkorporation, dem Staat nämlich, wird so das
ganze Volk zur Einheit und erlangt Individuation."

The State neither assumes nor renounces all functions of associate life; neither absolute centralization nor absolute decentralization is the normal political condition. " The central organs, from the government and parliament to the lowest administrative court, have a significance similar to that of the checking and co-ordinating centres of movement in the animal body." [1] They prevent the autonomous action of the subordinate associations and districts, the freedom of individual action, the competition between different parts, from destroying the unity of the whole. On the other hand, when the central organs devote themselves to minute details, and intrude upon the proper spheres of individual and corporate independence, there is presented both a symptom and a cause of an unsound condition, just as when a human being attempts consciously to direct his naturally reflex movements. The social aggregate-movement is not that of a machine—which is composed of manifold lifeless parts all deriving their motions from one central propelling power: it is a

resultant of countless initiating wills which, indeed, in the course of development, are evolved (*sich begeben*) under common rules and under the aggregate-organs of will and power, but which have surrendered, or can surrender, neither their particular spheres of freedom nor their participation in the central determinations. The higher the development of the understanding, feeling, and will of the members of the social body, the more will these members be found in paths serviceable to the general maintenance, and the more will they conform their movements to the requirements of the general maintenance, when conditions demand it. [2]

The central organs will thus be spared " many interdictions, regulations, ministrations, and applications of the aggregate-power."

[1] *Op. cit.*, p. 431.　　　　　[2] *Ibid.*, pp. 432–3.

The basal structure of the State is analyzed by Schäffle under the same five-fold classification of tissues that he found for society.[1]   There is, in the first place, the organization of political domiciliation and inter-communication (*Das staatliche Niederlassungswesen*) made up of the whole system of political localization and the transmission of political intelligence, the system radiating, through the public highways and other means of intercommunication, from its central point in the capital city to the sub-centres in the provincial capitals and its farthest branches in the local offices of the government.[2]   Corresponding to the second type of tissue, the State has its protective arrangements.[3]   These include such specific means of political protection and defense as fortifications, prisons, hospitals, forts, dykes, magazines, arsenals, ships of war and ammunition.   The arrangements for political metabolism—for public finance in the broadest sense, constitute the third type of State-tissue.[4] The management of the State income and expenditure devolves partly on special organs, but forms, furthermore, a part of the function of each institution.   In detail the State-economy is " the sustentation (*Ernährung*) of each particular tissue of which the State is composed."   Fourthly, the basal technical arrangements of the State comprise all means relating to efficiency in the execution of any of its functions.[5] Taken broadly, State-technique is " state-craft " (*Staatskunst*) or " politics " (*Politik*), and consists in " the establishment of a proficient personnel of service and the appropriate institutions: through instruction, training, practice, organization . . .   In a narrower sense, State-technique is the technics (*Kunstverfahren*) of the application of the use-

[1] *Op. cit.*, pp. 438–447.   [2] *Ibid.*, pp. 438–9.
[3] *Ibid.*, p. 439.   [4] *Ibid.*, pp. 439–440.
[5] *Ibid.*, pp. 440–1.

ful arts to State ends. The elements of this outer State-technique are the muscular endowment of the public servants (*die animale Muskulatur des Dienstpersonals*), and also factories, implements, weapons, apparatus, materials." Finally, the basal arrangements of the intellectual activity of the State are constituted of the means requisite to the intelligent determination of the ends and methods of the State-work and to the scientific direction of its execution.[1] These means are of two classes—one comprising the passive, the other the active, elements. The passive elements are the " symbols " (*Symbole*) for the expression, communication, preservation, and tradition of political ideas: these symbols include verbal communications, addresses, *etc.*, as well as written or printed reports, instructions, orders, and other documents. The drawing up, reproduction, preservation, communication, and tradition, of these symbols is accomplished through secretarial offices, reportorial organs, codes, and archives. The active part of the intellectual state organization is " the *personal* in individuals, boards, and corporate bodies. who in government, legislation, and administration of the State, in political parties, in the political press, in political unions and assemblies, fulfill the intellectual work of the State." [2]

Combinations of these political tissues make up the " organ-system " of the State.[3] The organs of the State are, on the one hand, the constitutional holders of public authority, and, on the other hand, the political agencies which in various ways influence the action of the constitutional organs. These political agencies include political parties and individual men; their participation in the life of the State is effected through such means as the agitation and develop-

---

[1] *Op. cit.*, pp. 441–447.   [2] *Ibid.*, p. 442.
[3] *Ibid.*, pp. 447–466.

ment of public opinion, and, more directly, through popular demonstration, or petition. There are two principal classes of the constitutional organs: first, the magistracies (*Obrigkeiten*), and second, the electorate and the representative bodies. Each of these classes, furthermore, consists of two categories, the central, and the subordinate and local. The central organs of the magisterial class culminate in the government (*Regierung*) which is the " nucleus (*Einheit*) of bureaucratically constituted departmental-ministries and collegially organized central offices." [1] In order that the maintenance of the whole be accomplished and that the action of the State be unified, it is necessary that there be both central and peripheral organs of the general social will (*socialen Willenseinheit*), endowed with authority to exclude all resistance and with capacity to perform the functions of organization, adjustment, and support, — that is, with both " positive " and " regulative " duties.[2] For these purposes not only unity, but also power, is essential. " The magistracies, at the head of which is the government, are the directing (*leitende*) organs of the collective-will and of forcible (*machtvolle*) execution; . . . it is absolutely indispensable that the directing organ of the social will-determinations should be at the same time the exclusive initiating organ of execution. In this capacity of being the organs both of unity and of power the magistracies, especially the government, constitute the real middle-point of the State." [3] The connection of these organs of unity and power " with the consciousness, feeling, will, and power (*Können*) of the whole people," is effected through the organs of popular representation (*Volksvertretung*).[4] The action of these organs is, however, spiritual only, not

---

[1] *Op. cit.*, p. 447.   [2] *Ibid.*, p. 449.
[3] *Ibid.*, p. 450.   [4] *Ibid.*, pp. 458–9.

material or physical—they having no direct participation in execution. " Popular representation belongs to the spiritual central organization of the State life." [1]

This differentiation of the constitutional organs into two classes and each class into central and subordinate groups, should not, Schäffle explains, obscure the fact that the whole State-system is the co-ordinating organization of the aggregate life and action of a society. It is an erroneous view which attributes activity of the will and understanding exclusively to the representative organs, and regards the magistracies as merely executive; the former inevitably exercise influence over actual execution, and for the latter a certain degree of discretionary action is indispensable. As the distinctive and essential end of the State is unified (*einheitliche*) action, there must be a super-ordination in both classes of its organs; this is attained through the system of reference and appeal, and through the hierarchization of offices and representative bodies. [2]

The process of the genesis and development of States is, in all its features, an inevitable consequence of " the inner and outer struggle for existence " [3] which is inherent in the social condition. No stage in State evolution is a result of accident, invention, the will of despots, or contract among the members of the community. These agencies may exert an influence upon the manner of transition; they do not create any stage of the process. " Self-preservation impels the most primitive horde to combination in united will and action; the struggle for existence . . . causes smaller communities to pass into greater ones, States to coalesce with States." [4] The same natural law determines the constitu-

[1] *Op. cit.*, p. 460.   [2] *Ibid.*, p. 448.
[3] *Ibid.*, p. 434.   [4] *Ibid.*, p. 435.

tional form which the State assumes at any stage of its development. The constitution is " the synthesis (*Zusammenfassung*) of the political forces of society into an integral organ-system of common will and action." [1]   A determining element of the general character of the constitution is the form of government. The form of government is determined by the location of the actual power in the State. Where, as a result of social selection, an individual or family has attained and holds the position of power, the form of constitution—or government—is the monarchy. In a true monarchy the individual or family hold the political authority as a result of his or their superior actual power, not by virtue of an investiture of authority from a prevailing class or from the whole people. The tendency of political evolution is towards democracy; for in the inter-society struggle for existence that society is the most powerful contestant, other things being equal, in which there is the most nearly complete identification of the aggregate, with the individual, will and power, in which, therefore, there is the greatest extension of political capacity and, consequently, of political authority.[2]

Political predominance may be the result of either physical or spiritual superiority; but whether concentrated in a single individual or family, or pervading a class, or diffused among the entire people, it can not be improvised or decreed, conferred and withdrawn. " It is the product of the historical work of social selection." [3]

The weapons in this natural social process of inter-social and intra-social contest and selection are varied.[4]   They may be acts of violence—usurpation, *coup d'État*, revolutions, op-

---

[1] *Op. cit.*, p. 473.   [2] *Ibid.*, p. 475.
[3] *Ibid.*, pp. 515–553.   [4] *Ibid.*, pp. 553–4.

pression, confiscation, banishment.   They may be acts of deception and artifice—bribery, simulated virtuosity, pretended religious sanction.   The strife may be wholly within the limits of law (*Rechtes*)—like the peaceful controversies between different States or between interests and parties within the same State—terminating in some mutual compromise or in arbitration by some higher authority.   Whatever the form of the strife, its final consequence may be any one of three kinds—namely, the absolute defeat of one side, the further result being the annihilation, suppression, emigration, or escape, of the defeated side; or accommodation of some sort—compromise, mutual concession; or finally, combinations into a new whole—union, federation, annexation, mediatization.[1]

The origin and development of the State thus exhibit the general law of social selection.   The smallest events of political change, as well as the great facts of origin, growth, transformation, decline, and dissolution of States, are all instances of that law which manifests itself variously with different nations and in different epochs.   The struggle —especially in its intra-society aspects—becomes less violent and destructive with the advancing development of any given social aggregate, adjustment replacing annihilation in the termination of the successive conflicts, and intellectual pre-eminence becoming more potent than physical superiority.[2]

From the history of national evolution—of the advance of an enduring social aggregate, we discover that there are five stages in the development.[3]   These stages are as follows: first, the primitive kinship group—the tribal and patriarchal

---

[1] *Op. cit.*, pp. 554-5.   [2] *Ibid.*, vol. i, pp. 292 *et seq.*
[3] *Ibid.*, pp. 279-283.

societies; second, the feudal society; third, the city-state community; fourth, the territorial community (*Landesgemein-wesen*); fifth, the modern national society. As a people attains " indivisible unity, collective individuality " in the State,[1] the stages of the constitutional evolution of the State reflect most clearly the more general social development.[2] The five constitutional stages [3] are: first, the primitive patriarchal constitution; second, the class-constitution—military, priestly, feudal, monarchical; third, the city-state constitution; fourth, the territorial constitution; fifth, the modern national constitution. "The general law of increasing differentiation and correlative integration dominates the progression of the successive stages: separation from a lower stage, and recombination of various separate formations of the lower stages into a higher unity as the next stage." [4] But (as pointed out by Defourny [5]) the particular criterion of gradation is not the same throughout. The first three stages designate degrees of complexity of organization and specialization of function rather than degrees of magnitude. On the other hand the territorial polity is distinguished from the city-state chiefly by size; it is a federation of cities each of which preserves its former constitution. But again the national-state is distinguished from the territorial-state by its inner organization rather than by size; it is a more highly organized territorial community.

5. WORMS

Among French sociologists no one has adhered to the

[1] *Op. cit.*, vol. ii, p. 556.

[2] *Ibid.*, pp. 552-591.

[3] *Ibid.*, p. 557.   [4] *Ibid.*, p. 556.

[5] *Cf.* Defourny, " Schäffle: son système sociologique, économique, et politique," in *Revue sociale catholique*, vol. viii, 1903-4, pp. 107-117.

biological method more consistently and completely than René Worms, who stands with Spencer and Lilienfeld in this respect. The greater part of his *Organism and Society* (1896) [1] is devoted to a specific account of the analogies existing between societies and organisms, the similarities being traced with regard, successively, to structure, functions, evolution and pathology. As preliminary to this detailed comparison, Worms gives, in the introductory chapters, an analysis of the conception of *organism* in order to indicate the essentiality of all the elements of that conception to the idea of *society*. Society is defined as "an enduring aggregation of living beings, exercising all their activity in common." [2] It is thus to be distinguished from fortuitous and ephemeral assemblages of persons, as well as from those more permanent groupings—commercial, scientific, philanthropic, *etc.*—the members of which are associated and mutually influenced with respect only to a part of their natures. Society thus conceived "is constructed on the same general type as the organism," [3] the social grouping (*groupement*) is "analogous to that of the cells of an organism." [4] The definition of an organism as "a living whole composed of parts themselves living" applies equally to society. [5] It is composed of living parts—human beings —and is itself a living whole, having its own life.

But holding that the difference between the inorganic and the living, or organic, can not be stated, nor the organic adequately defined, in a single synthetic formula, Worms proceeds to analyze the nature of the organic through a successive determination of the attributes by which the dis-

---

[1] *Organisme et société.*

[2] "Un groupement durable d'êtres vivants, exerçant toute leur activité en commun." *Ibid.*, p. 31.

[3] *Ibid.*, p. 30.   [4] *Ibid.*, p. 32.   [5] *Ibid.*, p. 38.

tinction between the world of life and the world of inanimate matter can be marked.   These distinguishing properties are then discovered each to pertain to society and to constitute an essential characteristic of its nature.[1]

In the first place, the external structure of an organism is variable in time and irregular in form, as contrasted with the constant and mathematically definite outer morphology of an inorganic body.[2]   The contour of society discloses a similar mutation in time and lack of geometrical definiteness.[3]   Its exterior form is determined by the territory which it occupies; the boundaries of this territory follow the " most capricious lines " and are continually modified by war or colonization.   "Absence of regularity in space, absence of stability in time, are then two traits common to the exterior form of society and that of the organism."

Secondly, there is a distinction as to internal composition, that of an inorganic body being relatively stable as contrasted with that of the organism, which is undergoing continual changes through assimilation and integration and the converse processes of disassimilation and disintegration.[4] Moreover, whatever change in mass the inorganic object undergoes is through superficial aggregation of the same or similar materials, while organic aggregation is through internal intussusception and transformation of dissimilar substances.   The character of loss of substance is likewise different in the two classes of bodies; inorganic loss being superficial and generally caused by external agencies, while organic losses are caused by normal internal functioning.   This distinction as to degree and nature of the mutation of composition constitutes the fact of nutrition—a

[1] Ch. i: " Définitions et comparaison générale de l'organisme et de la société."

[2] Ibid., pp. 19-20.   [3] Ibid., pp. 38-9.   [4] Ibid., pp. 20-22.

function peculiar to organisms. This double organic movement of intake and discharge, assimilation and dis-assimilation, is present in society.[1] At every instant society, acting upon the exterior environment, acquires new elements and converts them into materials of social sustenance. This social nutrition, consisting in the transformation and absorption of objects of the environment, brings about the formation of new vital elements of social life. " The development of wealth enables the members of society to increase their vitality and favors their reproduction. In that way new individuals are procreated and come to take the place of those who disappear. The movement of intake and discharge is thus double in society : there is an intake and discharge of goods (*biens*) and an intake and discharge of individuals. Each contributes equally to social life."

Nutrition not only is made possible by, but also subserves and promotes, the interdependence and co-ordination of dissimilar parts. This is a third organic quality—contrasted with the homogeneity or unco-ordinated heterogeneity of internal structure in an inorganic object.[2] There is differentiation among the human beings in society as among the cells of an organism ; social differentiation in its more elementary form manifesting itself in the division of labor.[3] Increase in the number of cells, the differentiation of various groups of these, and the specialization of structure and function, characterize social, as well as individual, organic evolution.

A consequence of nutrition constitutes another distinguishing attribute of organisms—namely, the function of reproduction, a phenomenon foreign to inorganic nature.[4] This characteristic forms a compensation for the subject-

[1] *Op. cit.*, p. 39.
[3] *Ibid.*, pp. 29–40.
[2] *Ibid.*, pp. 22–4.
[4] *Ibid.*, pp 4–27.

ness to death, which is, finally, a peculiarity of organisms. An inorganic body being simply a juxtaposition of elements and its individuality pertaining rather to the substance of its elements than to their union, a disjunction of the elements " works no great change in the pre-existing state " of the body. In an organic being, on the other hand, individuality pertaining to the *ensemble*, with a rupture of the bond which unites the elements the individuality of the whole is destroyed—there is death. A society is likewise subject to death, but, like the individual organism, escapes total destruction through its ability to reproduce itself in new societies which perpetuate its spirit and inherit its blood, its civilization, ideas and beliefs.[1] " The Roman society perished with the destruction of the empire of the West and the capture of Rome by the Barbarians; but in a certain way it still continues and survives in the Neo-Latin societies of western Europe."

Worms devotes a chapter to the refutation of the objections offered to the organismic theory of society.[2] The most common type of these objections may be expressed in the statement " the individual alone lives " (*l'individu seul existe*) :[3] only the simple has life; life can not be attributed to a complex of individuals ; society being such a composite can not be said to have a life of its own. The modern scientific view of organic life, however, removes all basis from such objections.[4] For every individual plant or animal is recognized as being a very complex composite of living parts, the ultimate organic elements which scientific

---

[1] *Op. cit.*, p. 40. For further discussion of the function of social reproduction, in its two forms of " organic " and " sexual ", *cf.* ch. xi.

[2] Ch. ii: " Objections et réponses."

[3] *Ibid.*, p. 43.   [4] *Ibid.*, pp. 43–46.

analysis is able to reach being each endowed with those properties which make up the conception of life. There is in animate nature only " unification," not " unity," or there is " unity of composition," not " unity of essence."

Another objection urged against the organic character of society is that contiguity and continuity, present in the natural organism, are absent in society.[1] Here again, a correct conception of the interrelations within society and organism, respectively, affords a two-fold refutation of this objection.[2] The only essential results of the supposed absolute contact of parts in the natural organism are the inner continuity of movement and of cause and effect, and the interchange of utilities. These results are produced for society through the physical similitude and mental homogeneity among its elements and the resulting economic interdependence, identity of language, government, religious and moral ideas, culture, and tradition. " It matters little, after all, whether two beings do or do not touch in space, provided that movement can pass from one to the other, and that what of utility is produced by the first is immediately communicated to the second and utilized by it."[3] As a matter of fact, however, there is no actual contact of vital parts even within plant or animal. There are intervals between cells as well as between the granulations of a cell, and if the proportionate dimensions of these intervals to the size of the cells be considered, they are found to be relatively as large as the ordinary spaces separating the members of a society.[4]

Finally, it is maintained that in the individual organism consciousness is concentrated in the nervous system, whereas in society it is diffused among its elements. A distinction

[1] *Op. cit.*, p. 46.
[2] *Ibid.*, pp. 46–50.
[3] *Ibid.*, p. 55.
[4] *Ibid.*, p. 58.

between the elements of society and the natural organism, respectively, exists in this respect; but that this is " not an absolute " distinction may be proved from two points of view.[1]   In the first place, a great part of the activity of even a man is unconscious; not only are his periodic physiological and respiratory movements normally unaccompanied by consciousness, but also many of his habitual operations, consciously directed at first, come in time to be executed unconsciously.   In the second place, the assumption that cells which do not form a part of the nervous system are totally devoid of consciousness is incorrect.   A rudimentary consciousness is indicated, for example, in the selective activity manifested by the humblest of such cells in choosing from the mass of nutritive materials conveyed by the blood just those substances which are proper to their needs.   This fact is further confirmed by the consideration that animals below the stage where differentiated nervous cells appear continually perform such discriminative actions as attest the existence of some rudimentary faculty of discernment.   " We conclude, then, as no naturalist would hesitate to do, that at the basis of every living cell slumbers a consciousness, which may only rarely and very feebly be awakened, but which exists, nevertheless.   No reason can be given ·to refuse totally to some what one is forced to concede to others. Where life exists, there can not be absolute unconsciousness." [2]

[1] *Op. cit.*, pp. 59–64.

[2] *Ibid.*, pp. 63–4.   In connection with the discussion as to the relative consciousness of the elements of society as an organism, Worms reasons that the distinction as to their relative freedom is likewise a qualified one.   By a deterministic argumentation of the usual type he shows that human free-will is merely human personality; that what of difference there is in the action of different human beings under a given set of circumstances is completely explainable by differences in their individual natures, hereditary and acquired. · *Ibid.*, pp. 64–8.

With this foundation of a general analogy between the individual organism and society, the remaining four parts of *Organism and Society* are devoted, respectively, to the "Anatomy of Societies," their " Physiology," their " Origin, Development, and Classification," and a social " Pathology, Therapeutics, and Hygiene." [1]   The analysis in each province is in biological terms and under biological categories, and the nature and taxonomy are throughout shown to be essentially the same in society and the natural organism. The cell of society is the human individual; the fundamental social groupings of individuals are the social tissues; and the systematic combinations of individuals from various groups into institutions constitute the organs of society.

Worms's final conclusion [2] from his detailed study of the resemblances of all phases between society and the organism is that there exists between them a " very profound and very close analogy," and yet not an identity of nature. [3]   As a consequence of the greater liberty and greater consciousness pertaining to the elements of society, there are characteristics of the latter which constitute more radical distinctions between it and animal organisms than any that exist between the latter and plant organisms.   The bond which unites the elements of society is chiefly psychic while the ligature within an organism is principally material. From this there results the higher degree of plasticity of society—the greater adaptability of its elements to varying functions—as a consequence of which when one social organ is destroyed, injured, or otherwise incapacitated, another set

[1] For a brief abstract, by Worms himself, of his organismic analysis of society, *cf.* his discussion of " la théorie organique des sociétés," in *Annales de l'institut international de sociologie*, vol. iv, 1898, pp. 296–304.

[2] *Organisme et société*, pp. 391–404.

[3] *Ibid.*, p. 391.   *Cf. Annales*, vol. iv, p. 302.

of social elements may readily undergo a structural differentiation which enables them to replace the inoperative organ functionally.   Finally, society is distinguished from the
natural organism through its greater complexity.   This results from the greater complexity of its ultimate element—
the human individual—as compared with that of the organic cell, and from the consequent greater variety in the
relations among its elements.   Though these differences, as
interpreted by the author in his concluding summary here as
well as in his refutation of objections to the organismic
theory of society, appear rather as distinctions in degree
than in kind, he yet considers them of sufficient significance
to mark off societies as constituting a third realm of being
—namely, the " super-organic " empire, as distinguished
from the inorganic and organic empires.[1]   The super-or-
ganism has the characteristics of organisms and yet additional characteristics; it is " *un organisme avec quelque
chose de plus.*"[2]

The State is a higher form of society; it is a society which
has become self-conscious and personal.   Every State is
necessarily a society; the elements of the State and of the social group at its basis are the same; both comprise the same
population.   But not every society has arisen to the form
of the State.   The State " is a society which has the knowledge and sentiment of its unity,"[3] and which has incar-
nated the idea of its unity in government and law.   Thus
" while society is an organism—or, at least, a hyper-organ-
ism, the State appears with the character of personality."[4]
The individuals are united not only by the racial, economic,
and moral bonds; there is here the " juridical and political "
bond also.[5]   It is in the State that the individuality of a so-

[1] *Organisme et société,* pp. 393-4.   [2] *Ibid.,* p. 394.
[3] *Ibid.,* p. 37.   [4] *Ibid.*   [5] *Ibid.,* p. 45.

ciety becomes clearly manifest, a characteristic which, as
already indicated, the opponents of the organismic theory
deny to society. Current language and a universal sentiment
with regard to the State affirm its individuality.[1]   It is
" a being having its own life, distinct from that of its members, though resulting from it; so distinct and so superior
that it at times demands the sacrifice of some one of those
subordinate existences, and almost always obtains it. Does
not he who sacrifices himself for his country believe in the
reality of the being for which he abandons his own life?
And if his act, in the eyes of all, passes for heroism and not
for folly, is it not because all, unconsciously or not, share
his belief? " [2]

This fact of the actuality of political society as a " real
being " (*être véritable*) is the basis for the first of the two
practical conclusions of a social-political character which
Worms, in his later discussions of the merits and aims of the
organismic theory,[3] bases on the principles of that theory.
With the acceptance of this theory " one will condemn that
radical individualism which would elevate each human being
into a being all-sufficient in himself, since one will have established, against that policy, the reality of the collective
being, and the necessity of an indissoluble connection among
all its elements." [4]   From the reality of the life of society
as a collective being follows the second principle of the organismic theory—namely, that society is subject to the laws
of natural development. The practical conclusion from this
principle means the discarding of the other extreme of so-
cial-politics, namely, " utopian socialism, which aims to reconstruct society on entirely new bases without taking ac-

---

[1] *Op. cit.*, pp. 45-6.

[2] *Ibid.*, p. 46.

[3] *Annales*, vol. iv, pp. 296-304.

[4] *Ibid.*, p. 301.

count of the natural process which has brought it up to its present evolutionary stage." [1]

In fact, finally, these two principles—that societies are " true beings " and, consequently, are subject, like all other things of life, to the laws of natural development—are, in Worms's later summary, the only essential objects of the organismic theory of society. Moreover, it is not claimed, he maintains, that the organismic method [2] is an exclusive method—for it recognizes differences between the organic world proper and the social world; and, on the other hand, it comprehends in itself, and reconciles with one another, the other sociological methods. " To admit that society is an organism is to say that its life is explained by the workings of those functions which predominate in the individual. But in the individual, thought is the highest function and nutrition is that function the fulfillment of which precedes all others." [3]   In the social life, likewise, there is the guiding principle of mind dealing constantly with the dominating physical necessities. The organismic theory thus has place for—and includes—the theories of " social psychism " and " economic materialism." [4]   And because in society, as well as in the domain of biology, some facts are at present beyond explication and require, therefore, simple declaration and verification without complete interpretation, the organismic theory needs also the methods of historical sociology. [5]

6. FOUILLÉE

The writings of Spencer, Lilienfeld, Schäffle, and Worms seem to exemplify with sufficient completeness the typical course of the organismic method in sociological discussion.

[1] *Annales*, vol. iv, pp. 296–304.   [2] *Ibid.*, pp. 302–304.
[3] *Ibid.*, p. 303.   [4] *Ibid.*   [5] *Ibid.*

It remains to consider, finally, a somewhat unique explanation of the social organism offered by an author whose principal work has been in other fields than sociology. This author is Alfred Fouillée, the French philosopher. Though Fouillée's analysis, set forth in *La Science sociale contemporaine* (1880),[1] shows unmistakably the influence of the sociologists—especially Spencer—there are, nevertheless, novel features in his interpretation. These features center around his attempt to harmonize, through psychological notions, the ideas of social contract and social organism.

Fouillée accepts, in its main principles, the theory of the contractual origin and nature of society.[2] On the other hand, he ascribes to society the essential properties of a living organism. He conceives society, therefore, as a "contractual organism" (*l'organisme contractuel*). The evidence of the organic nature of society he sets forth under two categories—the physiological and the psychological.

In his exposition of the physiological proofs,[3] Fouillée enumerates five characteristics of organic life, as follows:(1) concurrence of dissimilar parts, effecting the conservation of the living whole; (2) a systematized structure appropriate to this functional differentiation of members; (3) organic vitality of the elements; (4) spontaneity of movement; (5) evolution, or development and decay. In applying these points to society Fouillée presents nothing significantly new. He makes the familiar distinction between a mere cohabiting group of human beings and a society, properly speaking. In the analysis of structural organization, he adopts Spencer's three-fold classification of developed organic

[1] References here are to the second edition, 1888.
[2] *Cf. ibid.*, bk. i: "Le contrat social et l'école idéaliste."
[3] *Ibid.*, bk. ii, ch. i.

structure into the systems of relation or direction, circulation, and nutrition.   With respect to the vitality of elements, Fouillée holds that contemporary science teaches that each organism contains " a world of other organized beings " and that " every animal is composed of a great number of other, more elementary animals;" [1] consequently, " from the point of view purely physiological, every individual is a society and every society an individual." [2]

But from the nature of the elements of society Fouillée derives a property which plants and animals do not possess, and which pertains to the social organism alone ; this is the character of " interior finality."   In other words, in the social organism, the organic elements come to know and to will their peculiar function, namely, promoting the end of the organic composite which they constitute.   This peculiarity of the human social aggregate does not invalidate the conception of the social organism ; it simply makes of society a higher kind of organism.   " Human society has a superiority : the men of which it is composed come to recognize and to will the whole which they must form, the State in which all must live ; they can take for their end the common interest, and no longer the particular interest alone ; they can take for their end the social organism itself ; and this organism is realized by virtue of its being conceived [as an end]." [3]

The psychological characters of the social organism consist, Fouillée asserts, in the spontaneous attraction of the members of society for one another and in the " delegation of functions." [4]   The former property forms the psychological bond which unites individuals into a society.   In its origin this bond is the pleasure which individuals feel in the " in-

[1] *Op. cit.*, p. 83.   [2] *Ibid.*, p. 85.
[3] *Ibid.*, p. 91.   [4] *Ibid.*, bk. ii, ch. ii.

tellectual representation " to themselves of other individuals
of like kind. " It is a pleasure for every living being to
have around him beings similar to him which reflect in a
multiple way his own image and give to him a clearer perception (*conscience*) of himself, through the perception of
others." [1] The repeated experience of this pleasure develops it into a need. The bond of sympathy, intellectual
at first, " becomes finally a physiological impulse "—the instinct of sociability.[2] This instinct is developed and fixed
through natural selection and heredity. The society of
individuals thus united by instinctive sympathy of sensi-
bilities is fortified by a voluntary delegation of functions
on the part of the generality of men to a single one or
group, who are entrusted with the authority of direction and
protection.[3] The social nervous system consists of " all the
brains of the citizens." But only " the thinkers, the philosophers, the men who direct the nation by enlightening it,
those who govern it by requiring of it all acts necessary to
its security—only these are the social equivalent of the per-
fected cells of the brain." [4]

There is, however, according to Fouillée, no social brain,
properly speaking. Though society has psychological, as
well as physiological, marks of an organism, it does not
possess " psychological individuality." [5] There is no social
self-consciousness. The social consciousness is in no sense
a single consciousness; it consists only in the sum of the
social aspects of the consciousness of the individuals. There
is no social " ego." Society is not a " subject " that feels
itself and thinks itself. " Whether consciousness, consid-

---

[1] *Op. cit.*, p. 102.   [2] *Ibid.*

[3] *Ibid.*, pp. 104–5.   [4] *Ibid.*, p. 108.

[5] *Ibid.*, bk. iii, ch. iii: " La conscience sociale est-elle une conscience
individuelle ?"

ered in its absolute and metaphysical basis, is or is not composite, to constitute psychologically a single and individual consciousness there must be a gradation of concentration terminating in a subject saying ' I ' " [1]   Human self-consciousness is possible because the cells of the human brain are not themselves self-conscious units.   The very fact that the individuals of which society is constituted have each a consciousness of self precludes the possibility of a self-consciousness of which their consciousnesses are elements.[2]

The solidarity of different centres of consciousness in human States or in animal colonies may be very close and even indissoluble, but this solidarity does not involve a single consciousness or a complete fusion of consciousnesses.   What constitutes essentially a society, properly speaking, is the fact of being composed of feeling, thinking, and acting *subjects*— of subjects having each an ego more or less conscious and reflecting.   It follows thus that the social consciousness can not exist as a subject thinking itself, since its character of generality is incompatible with the individual character of every consciousness having an ego.[3]

There are thus, according to Fouillée, " three kinds of organisms : "

those in which consciousness is confused and dispersed (*a la fois confuse et dispersé*), as the zoophytes and annelids ; those in which consciousness is clear (*claire*) and centralized, as the higher vertebrates ; those in which consciousness is clear and dispersed, as human societies.   In the first kind of organism, a reflecting consciousness and an ego do not exist at all ; in the second, the elements do not have an ego, but the organism has one ; in the third, the elements have an ego, and, consequently, the organism can not have one ; there can [in social

---

[1] *Op. cit.*, p. 230.   [2] *Ibid.*, p. 243.   [3] *Ibid.*, p. 238.

organisms] exist among the consciousnesses only a unity of
subject, for it is precisely multiple subjects which, knowing
themselves and knowing others, associate themselves with reflection and freedom.[1]

The characteristic feature of Fouillée's organismic conception of society is thus his emphasis upon the absence of
a social sensorium.   In his interpretation the individual is
the only psychic subject of society, the only social personality.   The terminus of his interpretation is thus the idea of
the *contractual organism*,[2] " a more comprehensive idea "
in which he finds " the conciliation of the ideas of social
organism and social contract."   His elucidation of this idea
takes the form of a refutation of anticipated objections.

In the first place, he argues, though we find self-consciousness of the elements in the social organism only, this fact in
no way qualifies its character as a living organism.

Suppose . . . that our heart, our lungs, our stomach, our head
should each come to have consciousness of its proper function;
suppose that—while continuing to undergo the same sympathetic
reactions, . . . the same community of needs, the same necessity of reciprocal services—they should understand and accept that necessity in such a way as to accomplish voluntarily
what previously they were accomplishing fatally (*fatalement*) :
would life and the co-operation of parts disappear and the
body cease to be an organism?[3]

Fouillée considers that an affirmative answer to this question rests on two baseless assumptions.   The first is the
supposition that the various members would be able to sur-

---

[1] *Op. cit.*, pp. 245–6.   *Cf.* p. 402.

[2] *Ibid.*, bk. ii, ch. iii: "L'organisme contractuel, conciliation des
idées de contrat et d'organisme."

[3] *Ibid.*, pp. 111–2.

vive in separation from one another; to this he replies, simply, that the new element of consciousness would in no way lessen the dependence of each member upon the functioning of all the rest. The second is the supposition that the various members could not at the same time be " conscious of their function and persuaded of its necessity; ' '[1] or that they would divest themselves of their function because they were free to do so. The fallacy of this assumption he considers sufficiently indicated by the facts of political activity; though no citizen is compelled to undertake any part of the work of the State, and each functionary is at liberty to abandon his rôle at any time, political functions are duly executed and the life of the State goes on.

In the second place, the introduction of consciousness and will into the origin and elementary constitution of society does not make society, in Fouillée's opinion, an arbitrary or adventitious aggregate. Here the conciliation rests on the interpretation of voluntary action. Freedom of human action means nothing more than action impelled from within, rather than from without; in other words, action resulting from the tendency of ideas to be actualized. Voluntary human action—interpreted thus as the " efficacious influence of ideas upon their proper realization "[2]—instead of constituting a disintegrating or capricious element, gives greater solidarity to social organization. Society exists because " ideas in general, and the social idea in particular, possess a real evolutive energy, like the embryo of a living being."[3]

In fact, at what moment does an assemblage of men become

---

[1] *Op. cit.*, p. 112.   [2] *Ibid.*, p. 114.

[3] *Ibid.*, p. 119. *Cf.* p. 118: "the representation of a thing is already the thing commenced, the image of a movement is the movement in the nascent state, the idea of society is the nascent society."

a society in the true sense of the word? It is when all the men conceive, more or less clearly, a type of organism which they can form through uniting themselves, and when they do effectively unite themselves under the determining influence of that conception. We have thus an organism which exists because it has been thought and wished, an organism born of an idea; and since that common idea involves a common will, we have . . . a contractual organism.[1]

In Fouillée's system, therefore, society is both a natural product and an artificial product.[2] It is a work—not of artifice, which is opposed to nature—but of art, which conforms to nature. It is a natural and living being because it has in itself the principle of its movement and change. It is a work of art because its reality exists in the thought of man; it exists because of that thought. " Politics (*politique*), in a society of beings endowed with reason and will, must be a work of art in order to be a work of nature, and the contractual organism is precisely the conciliation of the two things." [3]

This notion of the influence of the " idea " in the life of the social organism forms the basis for the distinctive political implications of Fouillée's interpretation.[4] For though he enunciated many of the common practical conclusions from the organismic conception, yet the importance which he assigns to will and consciousness in social action makes it possible for him to advocate political doctrines which are strikingly rationalistic and paternalistic.

Thus Fouillée explains, on the one hand, that because of the mutual dependence of the parts of the social body, the

---

[1] *Op. cit.*, p. 115.   [2] *Ibid.*, pp. 121-2.

[3] *Ibid.*, p. 122.

[4] *Ibid.*, bk. ii, ch. v: " Consequences politiques de l'organisme contractuel." *Cf.* bk. iii, ch. iv.

legislator must conform his operations upon any one part to the relation which all other parts bear to that part. He must even at times withhold rectification of an aberrant member, because of the effect which his interference may have in inducing a more serious disorder in other members. Any profound or comprehensive reform must be undertaken only if the movement in that direction has already been initiated by a spontaneous modification within the inner nature of society. " But what is conformable to the natural tendency of a society, is conformable to the general will." [1] Thus a reform must represent more than the will or interest of an individual or class; it must proceed from all, or at least from the majority. As a definitive consensus is generally unattainable, advances must be insured through compromise; traditions, customs, and prejudices must be given the means of orderly transition. Finally, changes must be made with deliberation; due opportunity must be given for adjustment of all parts to the altered conditions of action.

On the other hand, Fouillée argues that these principles of the " natural history " of political society do not utterly exclude revolutions from the realm of rational politics. A languishing or diseased animal may be dependent upon a " physiological revolution " for the continuance of its life; an intelligent being may through conscious resolution radically change the course of his hygienic or moral processes. Likewise, persistent social distempers may make a political revolution necessary. But " legitimate revolutions " are only those which give vent to forces long accumulated and which are thus still manifestations of the general will; the leaders of the movement " are such by a spontaneous delegation, and the movement itself, having become irresis-

[1] *Op. cit.*, p. 129.

tible, is no longer an artifice of the few, but a natural deliverance of all." [1]

Fouillée considers that Spencer gave relatively too great weight to the autonomous functioning of organisms.[2] Spencer's underestimation of the efficacy of " ideas " in the conduct of the higher organic individuals led him, by analogy, to restrict too narrowly the sphere of State action. The brain of man is not only a centre of reflex action and unconscious co-ordination. It is also a centre of intelligent and voluntary " initiative." Similarly the intelligence and will of the nation can through its organs of direction give expression to volitional ideals and control the forces for their realization.

The State thus in Fouillée's system has a comprehensive and exalted sphere of action. He does not, however, clearly define the position of the State in the social structure; by implication the State may be understood as comprising the " organs of direction " of society. The detailed political applications of his theory appear only in the chapters on penal and " reparative " justice.[3] These chapters do not concern us as they contribute little to an understanding of his organismic conception.[4]

---

[1] *Op. cit.*, p. 132. [2] *Ibid.*, pp. 143-145. [3] *Ibid.*, bks. iv. and v.

[4] In the *Annales de l'institut de sociologie* for 1898 (vol. iv, pp. 169-339) is recorded an extended discussion, participated in by a number of prominent continental sociologists, on the question of *la théorie organique des sociétés*. Novicow, Lilienfeld and others argue in support of the theory. Tarde and Ludwig Stein are among the more notable of those who express dissent from the theory; Worms takes a somewhat conciliatory attitude (*cf. supra*, pp. 177-8). Novicow undertakes to answer the charges made by Tarde, Huxley and others that the organismic theory of society gives support to political despotism and paternalism. He also attempts to refute the various objections urged against the scientific validity of the theory; in this he follows the method of Worms (*cf. supra*, pp. 174-6), and makes free use of the idea that society is a par-

ticular sort, a "higher type," of organism. *Cf.* also his *Conscience et volonté sociales* (1897).

An interesting discussion of the organismic method appears in J. S. Mackenzie's *Introduction to Social Philosophy* (1890). Mackenzie confines himself strictly to a philosophical conception of organism. Defining organism as "a whole whose parts are intrinsically related to it, which develops from within, and has reference to an end that is involved in its own nature (2d ed., 1895, p. 164)," he argues that in that sense society is to be understood as an organism. He points out the irrelevancy of all accounts of analogies and similarities between societies and living beings. *Cf.* also *ibid.*, pp. 272 *et seq.*

For organismic sociological conceptions which are in general similar to that of Mackenzie, *cf.* Leslie Stephen, *Science of Ethics* (1882), ch. iii; and W. S. McKechnie, *The State and The Individual* (1896), pp. 8-26, 167-170, and ch. xviii.

For an interpretation of the nation as organism, set forth by an American political philosopher, *cf.* E. Mulford, *The Nation* (1870) esp. pp. 9-23, and 173-4.

CHAPTER V

CONCLUSION

It is somewhat difficult to subject the theories of the State that we have reviewed to any critical examination with respect to the validity of their interpretation of the State as an organic or personal entity.[1] Rarely is the argument supported by precise definition or carried out with careful reasoning. Even among those theorists who develop their conclusion through logical deduction there is no close approach to unanimity in their major premises. Nor do those who attempt to arrive at or substantiate their thesis inductively indicate the same kinds of facts or the same points of analogy as data for their conclusions or as verifying instances of their assumptions.

The variety of these theories is to be attributed partly to the variety of motives which led the thoughts of the different authors to the idea of State-organism or State-person. The desire to combat the theories which regarded the State as the creation and tool of man was the dominant aim of the earlier writers of the century, and was an underlying mood of perhaps all. Added to this motive among some of the later writers—notably Bluntschli and certain of the exponents of the theories of ethical organism and State-per-

---

[1] For the purposes of this chapter it seems unnecessary to deal separately with society as distinct from the State. The conclusions broached with respect to the organismic conception of the State apply without essential qualification to that of society.

445]   191

sonality—was the National-State idea.   As conceived by them the State was in some way the embodiment of the Nation.   The basis of the State was a naturally homogeneous people, united by common descent and the resulting community of ideas, traditions, and emotions.   Thus the State-organism was explained as the unconsciously evolved organization whereby the unity of the Nation was maintained, and the National will given unified expression and execution.   State-personality was regarded as being attained when a National self-consciousness had developed and had revealed itself in the constitution.   The aims and methods of other theorists, notably the sociologists, appear to have had a more purely scientific basis—the desire to unify and correlate all fields of knowledge and experience.   Political facts, they felt, must be shown to be essentially like other facts, particularly like some set of facts which have been more completely synthesized and systematized.[1]

Although it becomes clear, when we estimate these theories either individually or as a group, that they are somewhat deficient in exactness and consistency of method, we may still make a synopsis of certain fundamental properties which in all are either expressly or by implication ascribed to the State as living organism or person.   On this basis it will be possible to suggest certain conclusions as to the verity or worth of the conceptions.

In philosophical discussions the term organic has had a broader application than to the phenomena of biology, and this extension has often been deliberately adopted with the object of providing some general category that should embrace plants and animals as well as particular things which were to be newly designated as organisms.   Under the

[1] *Cf.* on this point Michel, *L'Idée de l'État*, pp. 473-4.

conception in this more general sense the essential characteristics of an organism relate principally to its end, its
structural and functional articulation, and its genesis and development.   The theories that we have considered undertake
to describe the State as organic from these points of view:
it is an organism because the explanation of its end, its
structure, and its evolution is to be sought within the
State itself.   The State is itself, they hold, the end of its
existence; to regard it as an instrument of something else,
is false and pernicious.   Its organic unity consists in the
fact that its structure is so specialized as to conform to the
character of self-end of the whole.   By this is meant the
distribution of component members into functionally differentiated parts, so that not only are the parts interdependent
and inseparable, but the whole is essential to the parts and
their elements.   Finally, the organic nature of the State's
evolution appears in the fact that in its origin and development it is "natural" and "necessary."   Its coming into
existence is independent of any external will, and the course
of its evolution can not be forced or deflected.   This does
not mean that the State is independent of the influences of
external circumstances.   The natural determinateness of its
history, its resistance to arbitrary transformation by man,
consists not only in the peculiarity of its inner relations, but
also in its constant dependence upon its environment.   Harmony with the "natural" circumstances of geography, race,
and civilization, is a condition of the continued existence of
the State.

But our study has been chiefly of writers who did not
stop with the ascription to the State of those more general
organic properties.   They maintained that the State is radically kin to "natural" organisms, or to persons; that it is
characterized by the essential property which differentiates
plants and animals and human beings from other objects.

The State was thus said to be a *living* entity. With the writers who conceived this life as primarily physical (or according to the biologist's conception, and as distinguished from psychic life) the evidences of the State's life were commonly found in the instruments and modes of its corporate action, and in the nature of its total growth. These writers described the "tissues" of the State-structure, depicted its systems of nutrition and circulation, and indicated organs fulfilling specifically the functions of brain, nerve fibres, heart, muscles, *etc.*; some found in the State even such organs as stomach, navel, or nose. The natural-organic quality of its growth was explained in general from the standpoints of necessity, continuity, and successive adjustments to environment—in terms not essentially different from the more general interpretation of organic development. By other writers the life of the State was understood as peculiarly of a spiritual sort, and its animate nature as principally manifested in the characteristics of "real" personality — namely, self-consciousness, self-determination, and ethical nature, in addition to the attribute of self-end. In the preceding chapters we have set forth in some detail the various respects in which the State was declared to manifest the signs of physical or psychic animateness, and we have sketched particular phases of parallelization which the different authors sought to demonstrate to exist between the State and the living organism or personal individual. It seems hardly important to take up these points in detail in order to examine their validity or show their fallacies. The two related theories, to sustain which those points were adduced, may be adequately estimated through an examination of their central propositions.

As to physical life, to criticise positively the proposition that the State is a living organism would take us into the most intricate part of biology. But a reasonable judgment of such comparisons as have been made may be reached without going into a detailed inquiry as to the biologist's conception of life. We are relieved from this task because the theorists who have attributed life to the State have not substantiated their hypothesis by any such analysis. Their comparisons have been all of an external sort. To give meaning to their statement that the State is living, they should have determined the nature and action of the elementary political units in their relations to the genesis and life of the State. The scientific significance of the predicate "living" seems unquestionably to depend upon its attribution to objects which not only react integrally and adaptively upon the environment, but also are evolved in a peculiar way and are constituted of structural and functional units manifesting certain peculiar reactions and undergoing, in the evolution of the objects, certain peculiar processes of multiplication and transformation. The theorists should have undertaken to demonstrate the genesis of the State-organism from its original elementary unit through the multiple divisions and subdivisions of the latter, and through the subsequent gradual differentiation of the unit products of those divisions, whereby different derivative units assume certain structural and functional positions in the economy of the State-whole. In other words, so long as the essential identity of the State with the physical organism is sought, the ultimate explanation of the life of the former must be made to accord with the established principles of the science of the latter. A living thing is distingushed from a non-living thing radically through the nature and action of its elementary units in their relation to the genesis, growth, subsistence, and coherent action of the composite which they constitute. Yet none of the theorists who have maintained that the State is a living organism have demonstrated any such rudimental similarity between the two objects which they thus associate. In discussing the organic growth of the State they have pointed out that the State undergoes a gradual modification in its form and *modus operandi*, and that the successive changes in general follow one dominant tendency; but what of normality was shown appears to be nothing more than that the successive conversions have been in conformity to the changing needs of the people, as conditioned by changing culture and environment; and they indicated no significant evidences of spontaneity and periodicity in that growth.

Furthermore, as far as the theory that the State is a living organism involves the hypothesis that the State has organic individuality, the question as to whether an individual organism can be constituted of individual organisms is important. The idea of the individuality of an organism seems incompatible with the thought of its being a constituent element of another organism, or with the thought of its being composed of organisms.   On the one hand, however dependent its existence may be upon the combined activities of an habitual group of individuals similar to it, its organic individuality seems to imply a functional completeness in its assimilative utilization of the benefits rendered by its associates, individually or collectively.   On the other hand, however dependent it is upon the combined functioning of its own elements, its organic individuality seems to imply that the complete cycle of organic functioning is not synchronously duplicated within its system.   The State can not, therefore, be explained as an organic individual if it has constituent elements which are organic individuals.   The term must be withdrawn either from the State or from the human beings.[1]

---

[1] On the question of the individuality of the State, *cf.* Driesch, *Science and Philosophy of the Organism* (Gifford Lectures, 1908). He expresses

Even, however, if this point be not insisted upon, and it be conceded, for example, that both the coral-colony and the minute animals of which it is composed possesss organic individuality, or that the germ cells of an animal are themselves organisms,[1] still organic individuality can not be asserted of the State in its relation to its citizens. However necessary to man's existence political residence may be considered to be, his absolute autonomy (so far as his character as a complete human being is concerned) in withdrawing from one State and associating himself with another contradicts the idea of the organic individuality of any given State-aggregate in relation to the men within it. The question of the organic individuality of the State is not a minor point or apart from the main hypothesis that the State is a living organism; this is evident if we reflect that the organismic theory implied to its adherents the dominating integrity of the State in its relations to its constituent citizens, and the inseparableness of the latter from the State, of which they were natural and vital elements.[2]

As to the psychic or personal life, leaving unconsidered the question whether we have any experience—or even any

the view (pp. 344-5) that there is no "positive right at present to maintain that any group of cultural or historical phenomena is more than a cumulation of the actings of psychoidal and moral individuals. We quite certainly know nothing at present about such a unity. . . . We do not see any complication or progress in human history that might not be explained as a cumulation in the easiest way. As far as we *know*, the State—in the widest sense of the word—is the *sum* of the acting of all individuals concerned in it, and is not a real 'individual' itself." *Cf.* also *ibid.*, p. 118, and Jellinek, *Allgemeine Staatslehre*, pp. 146-7.

[1] *Cf.* E. B. Wilson, *The Cell in Development and Inheritance* (New York, 1900, second edition), pp. 58 *et seq.*, 291.

[2] This does not mean that all these writers expressly compared the citizen to the organic cell or assigned him any specific place in the State-structure.

definite notion—of such a concept unassociated with some co-existent manifestation of animateness in the biological sense, it seems clearly incompatible with any distinctive conception of a psychic entity, or a *real* [1] personality, to attribute consciousness and self-motived activity to their parts or elements. And yet no theorists have denied that these properties pertain to the human persons within the State. What we have said as to organic individuality applies in like manner to the question of personal or psychical individuality, and to the untenability of the opinions which ascribe such a character to the State.

In view of the failure of the theorists to give rational basis to their thesis through a fundamental analysis of the sort above indicated, it seems unnecessary to point out in detail the absence of consensus in their selection of features of similarity, or to direct particular attention to instances of the use of ambiguous phraseology, of analogies which are obviously defective or vague, and of comparisons which are superficial or trivial. Even were the several schemes of parallelization between State and living organism or person consistent with one another, an analogy constructed in selected external aspects, or even an apparently complete morphological representation, would have no scientific significance. The value of such a system as an illustrative expedient would depend upon its appeal to an imagination of similar type to that of the artificers.

But may we, discarding the element of specific physical or psychic animateness from our conception of organism, retain the term as the most appropriate designation of the State because of its interdependent and functionally coordinated structure, the relation of its " end " to its existence and development, and the nature of its evolution—

---

[1] As distinguished from juristic or fictitious personality.

inevitable in typical tendency, though qualified through the particular circumstances of environment? In connection with this inquiry it is convenient to consider the question as to the moral value or practical utility of the organismic hypothesis of State nature. Does it serve to impress upon our minds certain conclusions of practical politics, to shape our estimation of political occurrences which have taken place in the past or which may be projected in the present or future? For we have seen that in the more practical aspects of the organismic theories the general purport has been to antagonize arbitrariness and capriciousness in dealing with political problems. The authors, therefore, have laid stress upon the doctrine that the State is not a lawless thing. It has a nature and end of its own, yet stands in inescapable causal relations with all features of its environment, and consequently can not be abolished, created, or transformed in defiance of its nature, end, and connections with other things. The joint question is then: in what sense are such statements about the State true, and is it necessary or useful to associate such predicates with any organismic principle?

First, as to structure. It has frequently been pointed out, in the first place, that the most mechanistic view of the State is adequate to the interpretation of the differentiation of functions among appropriately constituted parts, and the consequent relation among the parts of mutual interdependence and supplementation in the execution of their offices.[1] In the second place, in what sense should the State-aggregate be considered as *essential* to its members? Not, it would seem, in the sense in which the elements of an organism are conceived to be explainable only through explaining their relations to the organic entity which they compose and in disjunction from which they *ipso facto* lose their characteristic

[1] *Cf.* Jellinek, *op. cit.*, pp. 144-5, 151.

quality.   However important the existence of the State may be considered to be for the security and welfare of man, and however dependent upon the agency of political institutions men may be in the achievement of their most common and constant purposes (or in the " attainment of their destinies "), the existence of man in detachment from the most rudimentary political organization is at least not inconceivable.

Secondly, as to the " end " of the existence of the State, no reasons were given by the authors to show that we may attribute to the State a peculiar end apart from the sum or resultant of the ends of its citizens.   They indicated no political occurrences that may not be explained on the basis of the latter motives.   The more the permanent importance of the State to man is demonstrated, the more clearly does it appear that the end of the State must be said to be the well-being of man.[1]   Moreover, it may be conceded that where men are engaged in the co-operative satisfaction of any of their more general and permanent needs, the institutional form through which this co-operation is executed should be regarded as more enduring than they; that is, through that institution the accomplishment of their predecessors has been transmitted to them, and there is accordingly a moral obligation upon them to recognize that it has an end apart from the interests of the particular class or generation which through a given period of time participate in its activity or enjoy its benefits.   It does not seem, however, that there is any rational or moral justification for designating this truth as organismic.

Finally, the evidences of political history are such as to lead us to interpret the *resistlessness* of State-development

---

[1] On this teleological explanation of the State-organism, *cf*. Jellinek, *op. cit.*, pp. 145–6, and Driesch, *op. cit.*, p. 119.

in such a general sense as to deprive the notion of any distinctly organismic meaning.[1] To differentiate and estimate the full potency of contemporary deliberated human agency in devising and effecting State-changes, is a difficult and highly subjective intellectual process. But we can not follow the reasoning of those who interpret political activity as more essentially deterministic in its character than any other phase of human accomplishment. To affirm that if political formations are to be enduring they must be in harmonious correlation with such circumstances as past history, racial character, and the conditions of culture and physical environment, is not to posit anything peculiarly inevitable about State-development. Whatever men do is subject to like necessity. In all forms of human activity the means of successful effort are circumscribed by the nature of the end to be accomplished, by what has been done toward that end in the past, by the character of the medium within which the activity takes place.

If we examine the more particular practical conclusions which the theorists drew from their organismic premises, our opinion of the unserviceableness of the hypothesis is confirmed. We find that widely divergent applications are made. This is true, for example, with respect to their ideas as to the proper location of sovereignty in the State. Rohmer demonstrated, from the fundamental similarity of the State to man, that sovereignty should pertain to either the liberal or conservative, as distinguished from the radical and absolutist, classes of the population; Zacharia argued that the mechanical perfection indispensable to organic completeness requires that sovereignty reside in a hereditary monarchy. Frantz maintained that an aristocracy is the form of State pre-eminently organic; Schäffle contended

[1] *Cf.* Jellinek, *op. cit.*, pp. 148, 150; Krieken, *op. cit.*, p. 130.

from the law of natural selection, as applied to the State, that the goal of political evolution is democracy. Diversity of opinion as to the proper sphere of government likewise appears. Spencer derived his extremely individualistic views from the organic nature of society, and, as evidences of the organic character of political evolution, cited historical evidences of the constantly narrowing field of State-functions. Lilienfeld, on the other hand, set forth that an essential feature of the organic development of political society is the tendency towards stronger, fuller, and more varied activity on the part of the government.

In conclusion, it may be said that a final judgment of the theories of the State that we have considered depends partly upon one's agreement or disagreement with the authors in their understanding of the major terms of their theories. Our criticism, already broached, is as follows: the theorists failed to make explicit and definite their rendering of terms; certain fundamental propositions involved in their conception of organism or person can not be validly asserted of the State; such of their propositions as are valid are inadequate to prove that the State is organism or person in the sense either in which these terms are commonly used, or in which the theorists must be inferred to have conceived them; and the hypothesis that the State is an organism or person has no practical or moral consequence. This dissent from the general theory—whether as may be made up from the points of consensus among the different authors or in the form as developed by any one of them—is not meant to obscure the significance of important principles which were brought into view through the various elaborations of the central theme of the theories. These principles we may briefly summarize as follows: the close interdependence among the citizens and institutions of the State; the political effects of environment in its broadest sense; the consequences of antecedent

State events; the perpetual and important character of the aim of political organization in its relation to the career of man; and the relatively subordinate importance of any particular department of that organization. Associated with these truths we have the general practical doctrine that in all considerations of State-craft, in all plans for insertions, excisions, or revisions in State-organization, policies can not be expediently devised and executed in disregard of the conditions of national character, natural environment, past history, and the effects of changes in one part of the State-organization upon other parts; and, furthermore, that the end of the State must be kept in view and recognized as something beyond the temporary satisfaction of fluctuating demands of the present generation. In nothing that men undertake, however, are they independent of their past—in particular of what they have already done in that particular undertaking, of their environment, of the nature of the end to be attained, and of the consequences of one phase of their undertaking for other phases. In any step in an undertaking they work partly in ignorance of what their labor may bring forth, and of what consequences it may have for future generations engaged in the continuation of that undertaking. All this is simply a commonplace statement of the general causal interrelation of things. Neither the manifestness nor the intricateness of this interdependence within a set of phenomena which we may have synthesized on the basis of political quality, justifies us in attempting to integrate such phenomena into a concrete entity, and thereupon to attribute life to it, and designate it as organism or person.

Thus the important part of the work of the writers we have studied has been their insistent statement of what we may call the secondary principles of their systems. We mean to distinguish these principles, on the one hand, from the premise from which the authors sought to derive them, —namely, that the State is an organism or person; and, on the other hand, from the more superficial data which the authors alleged as evidences of their premises,—for example, that particular members of the State-organization or particular political operations are identical in nature with certain organs or processes, indicated as homologous, in the living organism or person. In other words, we consider that both the basis and the more superficial details of the system are invalid and superfluous. No dignity is added to the State by including it in the category of organism or of person, and the attempts that have been made to justify such inclusion have, as such, thrown no light upon the workings of political institutions.[1]

[1] For references to adverse criticism of the organismic theory, see *infra*, p. 209.

BIBLIOGRAPHY

I. WORKS OF AUTHORS CONSIDERED

Ahrens, Heinrich. Naturrecht oder Philosophie des Rechtes und des Staates auf dem Grunde des ethischen Zusammenhangens von Recht und Cultur, 1837. 6te Aufl. 2 Bde. Wien, 1870-1.
Die organische Staatslehre auf philosophisch-anthropologischer Grundlage. Wien, 1850.

Bluntschli, J. K. Gesammelte kleine Schriften. 2 Bde. Nördlingen, 1879.
Allgemeine Statslehre, 1852. Bd. I of Lehre vom modernen Stat. 3 Bde. Stuttgart, 1875-6.
The Theory of the State, Trans. by Ritchie, Matheson, and Lodge. 2d ed. Oxford, 1892.

Comte, Auguste. Cours de philosophie positive, 1830-42. 4me éd. 6 toms. Paris, 1877.
The Positive Philosophy. Freely translated and condensed by Harriet Martineau. 2 vols. London, 1853.

Eschenmaier, C. A. Normalrecht. Stuttgart u. Tübingen, 1819-20.

Fichte, J. G. Grundlage des Naturrechtes nach Principien der Wissenschaftslehre, 1796. Bd. III of Sämmtliche Werke. Berlin, 1845.

Frantz, Constantin. Die Naturlehre des Staates als Grundlage aller Staatswissenschaft. Leipzig u. Heidelberg, 1870.
Vorschule zur Physiologie der Staaten. Berlin, 1857.

Fricker, K. B. "Die Persönlichkeit des Staates" in Zeitschrift für die gesammte Staatswissenschaft, 1869.
"Das Problem des Völkerrechtes." Idem, 1872.

Fouillée, Alfred. La Science sociale contemporaine, 1880. 4me éd. Paris, 1904.

Gerber, C. F. v. Grundzüge des deutschen Staatsrechts, 1865. 3te Aufl. Leipzig, 1869.

Gierke, Otto. Das deutsche Genossenschaftsrecht. 3 Bde. Berlin, 1868-81.
"Die Grundbegriffe des Staatsrechts und die neuesten Staatsrechtstheorien" in Zeitschr. f. d. ges. Staatsw., 1874.

Görres, Joseph v. Teutschland und die Revolution, 1819. In Bd. IV
    of Politische Schriften. 6 Bde. München, 1854-60.
Hegel, G. W. F. Grundlinien der Philosophie des Rechts oder Natur-
    recht und Staatswissenschaft im Grundrisse, 1820. Bd. VIII of
    Werke. 2te Aufl. Berlin, 1840.
Held, Joseph. Staat und Gesellschaft vom Standpunkte der Geschichte
    der Menscheit und des Staats. 3 Bde. Leipzig, 1861-5.
Herder, J. G. v. Ideen zur Geschichte der Menscheit, 1784. 3 Bde.
    Leipzig, 1869.
Hertwig, Oscar. Die Lehre vom Organismus und ihre Beziehung zur
    Socialwissenschaft. Berlin, 1899.
        Allgemeine Biologie. Jena, 1906.
Krause, K. C. Fr. Das System der Rechtsphilosophie. Bd. II of
        Handschriftlicher Nachlass. Zweite Reihe.
        Leipzig, 1874.
        Abriss des Systems der Philosophie des Rechtes
        oder Naturrechtes. Göttingen, 1828.
Lasson, Adolf. Princip und Zukunft des Völkerrechts. Berlin, 1871.
Leo, Heinrich. Lehrbuch der Universalgeschichte. 6 Bde. Halle,
        1839-44.
        Studien und Skizzen zu einer Naturlehre des Staates.
        Halle, 1833.
Lilienfeld, Paul v. Gedanken über die Socialwissenschaft der Zukunft.
        5 Bde. Mitau, 1873-81.
        " L'Evolution des formes politiques " in *Annales de
        l'institut international de sociologie*, 1896.
        La Méthode graphique. *Idem*, 1897.
        La Pathologie sociale. Paris, 1896.
        Zur Vertheidigung der organischen Methode in
        der Sociologie. Berlin, 1898.
Mackenzie, J. S. An Introduction to Social Philosophy, 1890. 2d ed.
    Glasgow, 1895.
M'Kechnie, W. S. The State and the Individual. An Introduction
    to Political Science, with special reference to Socialistic and In-
    dividualistic Theories. Glasgow, 1896.
Mulford, Elisha. The Nation: The Foundations of Civil Order and
    Political Institutions. New York, 1870.
Müller, Adam H. Die Elemente der Staatskunst. 3 Bde. in 1. Ber-
    lin, 1809.
Planta, P. C. Die Wissenschaft des Staates, oder die Lehre von dem
    Lebensorganismus. Chur, 1852.
Post, A. H. Der Ursprung des Rechts. Prolegomena zu einer allge-
    meinen vergleichenden Rechtswissenschaft. Oldenburg, 1876.

Preuss, Hugo. "Die Persönlichkeit des Staates, organisch und individualistisch betrachtet" in *Archiv für öffentliches Recht*, 1889.

Rohmer, Theodor. Friedrich Rohmer's Lehre von den politischen Parteien, 1846. Nördlingen, 1885.

Schäffle, Albert. Bau und Leben des socialen Körpers, 1875-8. 3te Aufl. 2 Bde. Tübingen, 1896.

Schelling, F. W. J. Vorlesungen über die Methode des akademischen Studiums, 1802. 3te Ausgabe. Stuttgart u. Tübingen, 1830.

Schmitthenner, Friedrich. Ueber den Charakter und die Aufgabe unserer Zeit in Beziehung auf Staat und Staatswissenschaft, 1832. Bd. I of Zwölf Bücher vom Staat. Giessen, 1839-45.
Grundlinien des allgemeinen oder idealen Staatsrechtes, 1845. *Idem,* Bd. III.

Spencer, Herbert. The Principles of Ethics, 1879. 2d ed. 2 vols. New York, 1893.
The Principles of Sociology, 1876-80. 3d ed. 3 vols. New York, 1885-6.

Stahl, Fr. J. Rechts- und Staatslehre auf der Grundlage christlicher Weltanschauung, 1830-3. 3te Aufl. 2 Bde. Heidelberg, 1854-6.

Stein, Lorenz v. Handbuch der Verwaltungslehre und des Verwaltungsrechts, 1870. 3te Aufl. 3 Bde. Stuttgart, 1887.
Die Verwaltungslehre, 1864. 2te Aufl. (part). 8 Bde. Stuttgart, 1865-84.

Stephen, Leslie. The Science of Ethics. London, 1882.

Trendelenburg, Fr. A. Naturrecht auf dem Grunde der Ethik. Leipzig, 1860.

Vollgraff, K. Fr. Staats- und Rechtsphilosophie auf Grundlage einer wissenschaftlichen Menschen- und Völkerkunde, 1851-5. 2te Aufl. 2 Bde. Frankfurt, 1864.

Vorländer, Franz. "Die Staatsformen in ihrem Verhältniss zu der Entwicklung der Gesellschaft" in *Zeitschr. f. d. ges. Staatsw.*, 1859.

Waitz, Georg. Grundzüge der Politik. Kiel, 1862.

Wangenheim, K. A. v. Die Idee der Staatsverfassung, mit besonderer Rücksicht auf Württembergs alte Landes-verfassung und den Entwurf zu deren Erneuerung. Frankfurt, 1815.

Welcker, K. Th. Die letzten Gründe von Recht, Staat und Strafe. Giessen, 1813.

Worms, René. Organisme et société. Paris, 1896.
Discussion of "La Théorie organique des sociétés" in *Annales de l'institut international de sociologie,* 1898.

Wundt, Wilhelm. Völkerpsychologie. Eine Untersuchung der Entwick-
          lungsgesetze von Sprache, Mythus und Sitte.
          2 Bde in 5. Leipzig, 1900-8.
          System der Philosophie. Leipzig, 1889.
Zacharia, K. S. Vierzig Bücher vom Staate. 7 Bde. Heidelberg,
          1839-43.

II. HISTORICAL AND CRITICAL WORKS

Barth, Paul. Die Philosophie der Geschichte als Sociologie. 1ter Teil:
          Einleitung und kritische Uebersicht. Leipzig, 1897.
Bluntschli, J. K. Geschichte der neueren Staatswissenschaft, allge-
          meines Staatsrecht und Politik. 3te Aufl. München u. Leipzig,
          1881.
Bluntschli, J. K. und Brater, Karl. Deutsches Staatswörterbuch. 11
          Bde. Stuttgart u. Leipzig, 1857-67.
Bosanquet, Bernard. The Philosophical Theory of the State. Lon-
          don, 1899.
Defourny, Maurice. " Schäffle: son système sociologique, economique, et
          politique " in Revue social catholique, 1903-4.
          La Sociologie positiviste: Auguste Comte. Lou-
          vain et Paris, 1902.
Driesch, Hans. The Science and Philosophy of the Organism. Gif-
          ford Lectures, 1907-8. 2 vols. London, 1907-8.
Gierke, Otto. Political Theories of the Middle Age. Trans. by F. W.
          Maitland. Cambridge (Eng.), 1900. (A translation of sec. 11 of
          vol. iii of Das deutsche Genossenschaftsrecht).
Gumplowicz, Ludwig. Geschichte der Staatstheorien. Innsbruck, 1905.
Janet, Paul. Histoire de la science politique dans ses rapports avec
          la morale. 3me éd. 2 toms. Paris, 1887.
Jellinek, Georg. Allgemeine Staatslehre. Bd. I of Das Recht des
          modernen Staates. 2te Aufl. Berlin, 1905.
Krieken, A. Th. v. Ueber die sogenannte organische Staatstheorie.
          Leipzig, 1873.
Lewes, G. H. Comte's Philosophy of the Sciences. London, 1853.
Merriam, C. E., jr. History of the Theory of Sovereignty since Rous-
          seau. New York, 1900.
Michel, Henri. L'Idée de l'État. Essai critique sur l'histoire des
          théories sociales et politiques en France depuis la Révolution. 3me
          éd. Paris, 1898.
Mohl, Robert v. Die Geschichte und Literatur der Staatswissenchaften.
          3 Bde. Erlangen, 1855-8.
Preuss, Hugo. "Ueber Organpersönlichkeit" in Jahrbuch für Gesetzge-
          bung, Verwaltung und Volkswirtschaft im deutschen Reich, 1902.

Towne, E. T. Die Auffassung der Gesellschaft als Organismus, ihre Entwickelung und ihre Modifikationen. Halle, 1903.
Ward, L. F. Dynamic Sociology. 2 vols. New York, 1883.

III. SELECTED REFERENCES TO ADVERSE CRITICISMS

In general works on political or sociological theory the organismic conception has been attacked from various standpoints. The following passages are selected as being those which set forth more cogently the objections to the conception:

Barth, *op. cit.*, pp. 164-7; Giddings, *Principles of Sociology* (New York, 1896), bk. iv, ch. iv; Gumplowicz, *Geschichte der Staatstheorien*, pp. 436-475, *Outlines of Sociology* (trans. by Moore, Philadelphia, 1899), pp. 27-38; Jellinek, *op. cit.*, pp. 141-151; Edmond Kelly, *Government or Human Evolution* (New York, 1900), vol. i, bk. iii, ch. ii; Krieken, *op. cit.*, pp. 123-157; Leroy-Beaulieu, *L'État moderne et ses functions* (Paris, 1890), bk. i, ch. iv; Mackenzie, *op. cit.*, ch. iii; Michel, *op. cit.*, pp. 459-475; Gustav Rümelin, *Reden und Aufsätze* (Freiburg i. B., Dritte Folge, 1894), pp. 263 et seq.; Gabriel Tarde, in *Annales de l'institut international de sociologie*, vol. iv, pp. 237-260; Willoughby, *The Nature of the State* (New York, 1896), pp. 32-38.